Down Time

Ron Dentinger

Jokes compiled from his weekly *Down Time* column in

The Dodgeville Chronicle

KENDALL/HUNT PUBLISHING COMPANY
4050 Westmark Drive   Dubuque, Iowa 52002

CONTENTS

ACKNOWLEDGMENT

A special thank you to

Lois Argall

who played a big part in

putting this book together

INTRODUCTION

Humor's a funny thing. That isn't an attempt at being cute. Besides being funny/funny, humor is strange/funny. It is in that sense that I was referring to it. The "sense of humor" isn't understood by very many people. People like to laugh, and that's that.

It is difficult to describe why we laugh, but one thing is for sure, there is nothing else quite like it. There are few things that give as much pleasure as laughing does. One thing that does is: making people laugh. We all enjoy being able to make someone else laugh. That is what this book is all about. Now and then nearly everyone has to stand in front of a group and give a presentation or act as an emcee.

In the years that I've been on the banquet circuit I have seen speakers who use humor well, and I have seen speakers who misuse humor. It can work for you, but it can also work against you. Humor can help you to get and retain attention. Humor can be the spoonful of sugar that helps the medicine go down. It can help you to disagree without being disagreeable. With it you can make a point that will always be remembered. Misuse it and you can make an enemy who will never forget.

P A R T   1

The Uses and Misuses of Humor

I was waiting to board a plane in Philadelphia. Even in the City of Brotherly Love, an airport is a cold place to be. People tend to just go about their business. A guy sitting a few seats away from me had just bought a soft drink and had taken a big swallow. It obviously went down the wrong way because he started coughing and choking and a shower of liquid shot out from his mouth and nose. Nobody actually got sprayed, but you can imagine the guy felt rather embarrassed about the whole thing because everyone's eyes were on him.

It wasn't very hard to have empathy for his predicament; so I grabbed my umbrella, opened it, and held it between us. This got a laugh from him as well as from the other people who were sitting there. It changed the entire mood. It eased his embarrassment and lightened the moment for everyone. People started to talk to him, to me, and to each other.

Humor has a way of bringing people together. It unites us. In fact, I believe someone should plant some whoopee cushions in the United Nations building. The incident at the airport is an example of humor bringing people together. The result was what I hoped it would be. However, I could have bombed had I chosen to defend myself with a squirt gun rather than an umbrella. I might have been misunderstood, if not by him, then by the security guards. It's so easy to be misunderstood when you're using humor. If you don't remember anything else, remember that.

I would like to emphasize that humor can do a lot more than just entertain us. I believe that there is a place for humor in the work place. Let me take that a step further. I believe there is a NEED for humor in

1

the work place, if for no other reason than the positive effect it has on employee morale. Studies indicate that 15% of the people who lose their jobs, lose them because they don't have the proper job skills, but 85% of the people who lose their jobs, lose them because they don't get along with their co-workers.

Clearly good employee morale is very important on the job, and company executives should be aware that some daily humor can play a huge part in bringing about good employee morale. Some companies go so far as to put up special bulletin boards and encourage their employees to bring in cartoons and jokes to put on the board. This isn't an "anything goes" situation, but it shouldn't be too difficult to keep it in line.

Some Other Benefits

Too much of the dialogue that we encounter is predictable. This causes our minds to wander when we should be listening. Humor can make listening and remembering fun. That's why it's used in so many of our favorite TV commercials. That is also why it's used by most trainers and public speakers.

In the daily newspapers, it would take many words and much reading to make the same point that a political cartoon makes AT A GLANCE. Often mere words cannot make the point as well. We should use humor, when appropriate, in day-to-day business activities. The positive attitude brought on by humor helps an employee to retain the things taught in training seminars. A positive attitude can also help an employee to more readily accept the changes in company policy or method of operation. It can bring about an attitude adjustment that is nothing to laugh at. Humor is some powerful stuff, when used properly.

Using Humor Properly

The goal in writing this book was to produce a book that could not only entertain you, but also help you to entertain. More specifically, the book is for people who may want to use humor in a work-related way. Very likely that involves giving a presentation or being an emcee at a work-related function. Few people are very good at ad-libbing. Even those who appear to be ad-libbing are most likely pulling their lines out of a joke file in their heads. If you're with them long enough you will start to hear those same lines over and over. They say, "The best ad-libs are those prepared in advance." So you need to start your own collection of jokes. The jokes can be kept on 3 x 5 cards, and filed by subject, but you don't have to get that involved either. The method used is not important, as long as some method is used to start a joke file.

Visit the book stores. I especially like used book stores. If you find something you like, mark it with a highlight pen. Don't expect to find jokes that are "ready to use" as they appear in the book. It's better to look for jokes and lines that can be switched (re-worded) to fit your special needs. Switching from an old joke is one of the best ways to create a new joke. The more you do it, the better you will become. And best of all, the new joke is tailor made just for you.

Even if your joke file is nothing more than a box full of jokes on little slips of paper and some highlighted books, it will be useful when you go through it looking for ideas. The more you work on your joke file, the more you also build the joke file in your head. Soon you'll find that you too have a mental joke file that can be called on when the need arises. The name of the game is: ASSOCIATION. Before long you don't even have to call on your memory. It just delivers. Something triggers it, and the association begins. Out comes this joke, and everyone thinks that you're one of those quick thinkers who can ad-lib. At that point they will be right.

A Funny Thing Happened

Many of the bits used in my routine have actually happened. In the opening portion of the routine, I say:

"My wife said she had an accident with the car, but she said, 'Don't worry! I was driving the old car.'

I said, 'What did you hit?'
She said, 'The new car.'"

This actually happened to a friend of mine. Funny things happen to all of us, all the time. Your job is to look for them and write them down for possible future use. Keep in mind that it's not only okay to enhance your stories, it is actually smart to enhance your stories. You can make them better than they actually were. Go ahead...lie. It's okay.

3

Some Points About Telling Jokes

There are only a handful of people in the entire country who can tell a good LONG joke. There are some, but very few. Most people give detail that just isn't necessary. And the detail doesn't add to the joke. It detracts from the joke and dilutes the laugh. So just as you would in a business letter, you get rid of every word that is not absolutely necessary. Get down to just the words needed for the joke to make sense.

You'll find that there is a key word in the last line of every joke. In the punch line. The key word is going to stand out because it's the one word that is needed for the joke to be funny. The key word should be the last word in the joke. Even a word or two after the key word will dilute the laugh. So you sit down in advance and re-write the last line making the key word the last word. It can be done almost every time.

STRONG JOKE:
"Mommy, can I have a baby sister for Christmas?"
"There aren't enough shopping days left."

WEAK JOKE:
"Mommy, can I have a baby sister for Christmas?"
"There aren't enough shopping days left so I'm afraid not."

The difference may seem trivial, but take my word for it—the first one is better. Resist the temptation to be wordy.

If you use something that's new, even if it's an old joke, it's not enough to mull it over in your mind, and then try to deliver it, out loud, when you get up in front of the group. What happens is: there's a strong chance you're going to trip over your tongue. What you need to do (even if you feel like a fool talking to yourself, alone in your car) is to say the words over and over again—out loud—enough times so they flow smoothly. Then they should also flow smoothly when you get up in front of the group.

Understanding What Makes a Joke Work

Most jokes start out sounding normal, and then SUDDENLY there is an ABRUPT change in direction. It's important to know that the more suddenly and abruptly a punch line comes, the bigger the laugh is likely to be. On the other hand, the more you're able to see a punch

4

line coming, the smaller the laugh is likely to be. Don't forecast the punch line!

One of the things that makes a joke funny is exaggeration. You either over-state the case, or under-state the case, but either way you exaggerate the case. Like a magnifying glass makes something large enough that it can be more easily seen, the exaggeration in a joke makes the point of the joke easier to see and understand.

Point to be Made

It's not how hard you work, it's what you accomplish.

Using Exaggeration to Make the Point

An employee tells the boss, "I made 34 sales calls today. I could have made more, but some of the prospects wanted to know what I was selling."

Nobody is that dumb, but the joke exaggerates the point so it is very clear. Who cares how hard you work if you are not being effective? Enthusiasm without effectiveness is known as "Energized Incompetence." Exaggeration brings the point home.

Caricature drawings are funny because they exaggerate a person's faults. The caricature used in my brochure was drawn several years ago. I didn't look like that. I have since grown into my caricature. It's now more like a photograph. What once were exaggerated faults are now facts. (I thought you'd like to know.)

Categorizing Jokes Isn't Bad, But... ━━━━━

The jokes in Part 2 are not listed by category. There is a good reason for this. Many people who are going to talk to a certain type of group, will look for jokes in that category. For example: If you're going to talk to lawyers, you are likely to look for some lawyer jokes. This can be a mistake. The lawyers have heard enough lawyer jokes. And if you're not part of the group, you may not know what is taboo, and should therefore be avoided. Believe me, in every group there may be things that are sacred. Things that they "don't kid about."

Ron's Rule

- If you're talking to farmers, don't tell farmer jokes.
- If you're talking to doctors, don't tell doctor jokes.
- If you're talking to lawyers, don't tell snake jokes.
  (Summary: If you talk to doctors, tell lawyer jokes.)

Obviously, there are times when you customize to a group, but not as often as you might think. People are *first* people, and then they are whatever else they are.

Perceived Value

How humor is received, is every bit as important as how it is delivered. And how you are perceived plays a big part in how your humor is received. I wish this were not the case, but it is the case and you can't change it. You can, however, use this knowledge to your advantage. The pros are able to control how they are perceived by the audience. As a result their humor is likely to be well received by the audience. That is why they are "the pros." That is probably the biggest single thing that separates them from the amateurs. I can't tell you what to do. What works for me, probably won't work for you. I can only make you aware that "perceived value" is extremely important. People tend to "buy the box" instead of what's in the box. Again, I wish this were not the case, but it is definitely the case. You need to be aware of it.

Writing Your Own Jokes

Making up a joke is not as difficult as you might think. If you practice, you'll eventually start to "think funny." Your mind thinks logically. To write a joke you have to think randomly. There are methods you can use to force your mind to think randomly. The method I use is a variation of one that goes back to the days when gag writers wrote funny lines for radio shows. The method probably goes back further than that. My version is another step in this evolution. A sample is pictured here for you to use. You can start by drawing a reproduction of it on an 8½ by 11 inch piece of paper, and use it as a master from which you make your working copies on a copier.

Let's say that you want to write some jokes about your son going to college. You start to fill in words as they come to you. Under WHO

TOPIC:

	WHO	WHAT	WHERE	WHEN	WHY
RELATED					
EXPRESSIONS & PHRASES					
UNRELATED					

7

(on top) you might put: the teacher, the dean, a classmate, etc. The top is for related things. Don't try to be funny on top. The WHO, WHAT, WHERE, WHEN, WHY entries on top must be related to the topic. On the bottom is where you try to be creative. You look for words that aren't related to your son going to college. Example: Under WHO you might put: the plumber, the Avon lady, or someone currently making news. Under WHAT you might put: a Twinkie, a dirty sweat sock, etc. Keep doing this until you have five or six words in each of the top and bottom slots. In the EXPRESSIONS AND PHRASES slot you can use both related and unrelated sayings. For example: "This Bud's for you," or "It hurts when I go like that," or "He earns money the old-fashioned way." Try to be clever.

Now you are ready to create some jokes. Begin to look over the entire sheet. Randomly put together things from all over the sheet. As you do this, eventually you'll hit on an idea. That is the birth of a joke. At first the idea is weak, but you re-word the idea and soon it becomes stronger. Then write it down and go on to find others. Here is one of the lines I came up with using this method:

> The guy who sits behind my son told him that he had the answers to every question on the test, and would sell them for fifty dollars. So my son gave the guy fifty dollars, and the guy gave my son a text book.

Funny? I think so. But a line standing alone, won't deliver the same punch it will when it becomes part of the routine. Don't worry if you don't come up with "a real knee-slapper" every time you try to write. Nobody does. The more you write, the more often you happen upon a strong joke.

Packaging the Jokes

Put your jokes together in related groups of three. This is known as: The Rule of Three. Four is usually too many and two isn't enough. You then have a mini-routine which can develop the momentum that a single joke probably won't. The first one sets-up the second one, and the second one sets-up the third. You can often tell three short, fast jokes in less time than you can tell one long joke, and get a lot more laughter too.

If you are teaching or training, you should use only enough humor to be an effective teacher or trainer. Don't try to be a comedian. But if you are doing a retirement banquet, or the company's Christmas party, then string a few mini-routines together and do a longer (not long) routine. A strong five or ten minutes is much better than twenty minutes that starts to drag at the end.

Many of the jokes in Part 2 use the: "A guy goes into..." format. This works okay in print, but it's not the best way to tell a joke when you are presenting in front of a group. Personalize to the group. Use the person who introduced you. Use the person next to you. Pick on people who are well known to the group. Tease them; don't torture them. Don't use people who are too old or too young. Neither gets a maximum laugh.

Use a conversational tone of voice. It's important that you don't sound "canned." You should sound natural, as if you are just talking.

A Sample Personalized Mini-Routine with Natural Delivery

(Lead-in) I'd like to thank Bob Johnson for carrying the projector up from the 1st floor. He wasn't even winded. (pause)

(1st joke) Bob was telling that he still does 50 push-ups a day.... (pause) ... Not all at once. He falls down a lot.

(2nd joke) He said he was captain of his high school football team for seven years. (pause)

(3rd joke) He could run and he could kick...but he couldn't pass.

Some Odds and Ends

- If you can't be heard, you can't be funny. Use a good PA.
- It's hard get 50 people to laugh in a room that holds 550.
- Take small bites. First master 5 minutes, then 8, then 12.
- Open strong. It's hard to change a bad first impression.
- If you can't do dialects well, don't do them at all.
- If your "stuff" is funny, you don't have to act funny.
- You can't please everyone. Learn to ignore a lone sourpuss.
- If you have to solicit compliments, they're not compliments.
- Close on a high point, and stop while they still want more.
- It's easier to get a new audience than a new routine.

Boy Scouts are warned not to purchase Tates Compasses because they don't work. In fact, they are the reason for the old adage: "He who has a Tates (hesitates) is lost."

Another old adage: "The pun is the lowest form of humor. Many people think the second old adage understates the case. A little goes a long way when it comes to punning. Fred Allen once said, "Hanging is too good for people who make puns; they should be drawn and quoted."

My wife bought 20 pounds of Limburger cheese. That's quite a phew! I think the last one is only two-thirds of a pun. (Two-thirds of P U N = P U)

But seriously, word play (especially puns) is not the best kind of humor to use if you're talking to a group. A pun once in a while is okay in your normal conversation. It is okay even when written, but if another old adage, "More is not necessarily better," is true regarding humor in general, then it goes double for puns.

My Uncle Bob used to say, "If at first you don't succeed, the tough get going." (We spelled his name with two o's). Yes, it was from Uncle Bob that I learned the value of the phrase, "What are you talking about?" Sorry, I'm drifting away from what I actually wanted to say. Uncle Bob knew the exact day he was going to die, months before he died. How? The judge told him. You want to know what he did wrong? He told the following pun to a large group:

A guy complains to his doctor that he's been dreaming about talking mice, talking dogs, talking crickets and even talking ducks. The doctor says, "Nothing to worry about. You're just having Disney Spells."

The Tricky Part ──────────────

All kidding aside, puns are not bad. They just don't work. The real problem you'll run into when speaking to a group is: It's so easy to go too far. A President is doing great even if 30% of the people in the country hate him. I couldn't take that kind of rejection. But in a banquet or business setting I know I'm in big trouble, if I offend only 5% of the people. There is a line that you better not cross. Still, to get the hard laughs you have to get as close to that line as you can, without crossing it. The closer you get the harder the laugh. That's the way it works. That is the very nature of laughter, as a response to humor.

That sounds a little tricky doesn't it? Well, that's not the tricky part. The tricky part is that the line keeps moving, and at times it's almost invisible. Laughter is not automatic. What works in the local comedy club won't work at a banquet, even if the people, the material and the delivery are exactly the same.

How do you determine what you can do, and what you can't do? You have to develop sensitivity. If you are in doubt...don't! You have to know when to stop. Some people just don't know when to stop. There is nothing worse. Having made that point, I will make one closing point. There is nothing worse than those people who don't know when to stop, but if there were, it would surely be those people who don't know when to start. Those people who look to be offended, and take great pleasure in demonstrating how offended they are. Somewhere in between these two ugly extremes lies the balance we should shoot for. Both extremes want us to let their conscience be our guide. The world would be a better place if it had a little more in three areas. They are: moderation, toleration and laughter.

Suggested Reading

Heilitzer, Melvin. *Comedy Writing Secrets*, Writers Digest Books, 1507 Dana Avenue, Cincinnati, OH 45207.

Perret, Gene. *How To Write & Sell Your Sense Of Humor*, Writers Digest Books, 1507 Dana Avenue, Cincinnati, OH 45207.

_____. *Comedy Writing Workbook*, Sterling Publishing Co., 387 Park Avenue South, New York, NY 10016. (Published 1990, out of print)

Rapp, Albert. *The Origins Of Wit And Humor*, E.P. Dutton & Co. Inc., New York, NY 10016. (Published 1951, out of print)

The Origins Of Wit And Humor might be found in your library. My personal library includes hundreds of humor books. The Albert Rapp book is the best book I have found that looks at why people laugh. It is not a joke book. It is very interesting reading if you can find a copy. Also look for it in used book stores.

Down
Time

P A R T 2

The Jokes

I'm not saying my brother-in-law looks for sympathy...
but how many people limp when they have a cold?

A banker tells a few bad jokes and nobody says too much,
but just let a comedian pass a few bad checks...!

Grandpa says one of the nice parts about getting old
is that not only can you sing while you shower,
you can sing while you brush your teeth.

My wife's favorite song:
"IF YOU WERE THE ONLY BOY IN THE WORLD AND I WAS
THE ONLY GIRL OKAY, BUT OTHERWISE LET ME ALONE."

I overheard my wife on the phone saying, "Marriage is a lot like
eating in a restaurant. About the time you get what you wanted, you
look around and see what someone else has and kind of wish you
would have had that."

...then one year things got so bad in order to make ends meet I had
to sell the house. My family took it quite well but the landlord was
really mad!

Psychiatrist to telephone receptionist:
"Just say we're very busy around here, not this place is a mad
house."

Remember: "BOSS" spelled backwards is double S-O-B.

The most realistic toy item this past Christmas was the "Teenager Doll." You wind it up and it resents you for it.

Q: Why do grandparents and grandchildren get along so well?
A: Because they have a common enemy.

The biggest snow storm of the season hits town and the local first grade teacher spends twenty minutes tugging and pulling to put boots onto one of the kids. She finally succeeds only to hear the kid say, "Those aren't my boots."

Twenty more minutes of tugging and pulling takes place as the teacher struggles to get the boots off again. The kid says, "They're my brother's boots, but Mom makes me wear them."

He's not a connoisseur...he's more like a common-sewer.

I was going to write a book, but you can buy one for $15.95.

I took skiing lessons last year, but by the time I learned to stand up I couldn't sit down.

You can be pretty sure the magic is gone from your marriage when your wife continues to chew her gum while you kiss.

I asked Grandpa where he went on his honeymoon.
He said, "Upstairs."

Talk about being left handed...
The only thing I do with my right hand is wash my left hand.

For your information:
They're running out of speeding tickets.
So if you want one, you'll have to hurry.

Sure I'm worried about Zero Population Growth. There are too many zeros running around now.

———

Dumb? My brother-in-law has trouble UN-folding a map.

———

The landlord asks too much for the rent. It's getting bad. Last month he asked four times.

———

One morning my son interrupted our coffee with this beauty: "Today's Nerd Day at school. Can I wear some of your clothes?"

———

My uncle knew—six months in advance—the exact day he was going to die.
The judge told him.

———

They've somehow mixed up my post office box number with my Social Security number. Now I can't get my mail until I'm 65.

———

With mail like I get I don't need a letter box.
I need a litter box.

———

Nobody knew me until I got a brand new car. Then they'd say, "There goes what's-his-name."

———

I'm glad they didn't name me after my father.
Can you imagine going through life with a name like POP?

———

I'm humbler than you are and darn proud of it.

———

Talk about poor table manners. This guy eats with his fingers and talks with his fork.

———

When my wife and I travel together, she does all the driving.
All I have to do is turn the wheel and push the pedals.

———

"Waiter, this food is terrible...let me talk to the manager."
"Sorry, the manager isn't in."

"Where is he?"
"He's out to lunch."

———

Q. What ever happened to your beard?
A. I still have it, but I keep it shaved off.

———

Off-color song: "Rhapsody In Green."

———

When asked how he was doing with his new poultry operation, the farmer replied: The poultry business isn't so good for me, but my son is doing fine with it. I buy the chickens for him. I pay for their feed. Then I buy the eggs from him . . . and he eats 'em.

———

I had Claustrophobia so bad I had to move out of Rhode Island.

———

The town drunk is in court yet another time. The judge says, "I told you I didn't want to see you in here ever again!"
The drunk replies, "That's what I tried to tell the officer, but he wouldn't listen."

———

If you took enough cars and placed them bumper to bumper, so they completely encircled the earth, some idiot in a Yugo would try to pass!

———

How come people who snore always fall asleep first?

———

You think this is dull? You should see my love life!

———

Before you sign that contract...remember:
"The big print giveth and the small print taketh away."

———

My insurance policy coverage isn't hundred dollar deductible. It's hundred dollar debatable.

———

I was sitting in the smoking section of a Madison restaurant that had a very strict smoking policy. The waitress told me: "If you don't start smoking soon, you'll have to leave."

———

It doesn't make sense. They now say smoking is twice as bad for you than they used to say it was...and they used to say it would kill you.

The worst years of marriage are those following the wedding.

A salesman, cutting across a field to talk to a farmer, notices a large bull standing less than a hundred feet away. The salesman calls out to the farmer, "Is that bull safe?" The farmer calls back, "A lot safer than you are."

Girl to boy friend:
"My dad likes to take things apart to see why they don't go...so you'd better go."

"I'm here to tune the piano."
"I didn't call for a piano tuner."
"I know...your neighbors did."

Sign in a paint and wallpaper store:
"Husbands picking out colors must have a note from wives."

My dog thinks his name is Downboy.

I don't care what the TV ads say. You can't get a refund on lost travelers' checks, if you lost them in a poker game.

Unwritten law in Reno, NV: "A Colt .45 beats Four-of-a-kind."

I've got property in Las Vegas.
The Sands is holding my luggage.

Grandpa says, "It's too bad, but these days the word 'Honesty' is usually preceded by the words: 'Good Old-Fashioned.'"

I'm not saying that she has a big mouth, but when she smiles she gets lipstick on her ears.

WASTEBASKET: A handy container to throw things near.

In an attempt to diversify my investments, I got into the cattle business. I bought 10 female pigs and 10 male deer. As of this writing I've got twenty sows 'n bucks.

The city council got together and decided to do a few things to improve the image of the city, so they changed the name of the subdivision from Goat Hill to Angora Heights.

Next year we're going to send the dog to camp and the kids to obedience school.

A woman and her husband come into a local dentist's office.
The woman says, "I need to have a tooth pulled but I'm in a big hurry, so don't bother with the Novocain."
The dentist says, "It's much too painful without Novocain."
The woman insists, "I don't have time. Pain isn't important."
The dentist asks, "Which tooth do you want pulled?"
The woman says to her husband, "Show him your tooth."

I still do about fifty push-ups a day. Well, not all at once. I fall down a lot.

This morning I touched the floor without bending my knees. I fell out of bed.

Wife: "There is no hook in the bathroom, so I have to hang my robe on the door knob and it drags on the floor."
Husband: "All right, all right, I'll fix it. Bring me your robe and a scissors."

It must be February. My nose runs and my car doesn't.

My wife was going to try skiing, but she thinks it makes her feet look too big.

"I'm looking for the people who live here."
"Well, you've come to the right place."

Operator: "Please deposit ten, seventy-five."
Caller: "But I said I wanted the charges reversed."
Operator: "Fine! Deposit seventy-five, ten."

It would be so nice to be as sure of anything, as some people are of everything.

I'll never forget what's-his-name.

I had a bad memory...then I took that Dick Carnegie course.

"Does your wife know that you're bringing me home for dinner?"
"She should know...we argued about it for two days."

Guest: "It appears that your dog doesn't like me."
Host: "He's just upset 'cause you're eating out of his bowl."

Now there's a new computer telephone option you can order.
The computer can actually understand the spoken word, so you don't have to dial. You just speak the number into the phone.
As I recall...that's how it all started.

How come wrong numbers are never busy?

Did you know that in this town there are a whole bunch of married women who have no desire to cheat on their husbands?
I know. I asked them.

The older a man gets, the faster he could run as a boy.

They took football seriously at my high school. I didn't realize just how serious they took it. Then one year they traded me to Cleveland.

We had a small team. A very small team. In fact, the coach was only five foot nine inches tall and none of us knew he had a bald spot.

I was captain of the high school football team for 7 years.

First neighbor: "Can I use your lawn mower tomorrow?"
Second neighbor: "As long as you don't take it out of my yard."

First neighbor: "Did you get your gardening done?"
Second neighbor: "Yes, and I suppose you want your hoe back?"
First neighbor: "I don't...but the guy I borrowed it from says the owner wants it."

RECIPE FOR SPONGE CAKE: Borrow 1 cup of milk. Borrow 3 eggs. Borrow 2 cups of flour. Borrow a cup of sugar. Borrow a...

I never know what to get my wife for Valentine's Day.
I was going to get her a book, but she already has one.

Last year she got me one of those expensive eight-day clocks.
The instructions say it will go eight days without winding.
Can you imagine how long it would go if you wind it?

The owner of one of the stores in town complained that people constantly stop in for no other reason than to ask him what time it is. So he bought a clock and put it in his window. Now they stop in and ask, "Is that clock right?"

You know what is really frustrating?
Arguing with someone who knows what they're talking about.

A guy works his way to the front of a crowded convention hall and hollers out, "I've lost my wallet which has $850 in it, and I will give $25 to anyone who turns it in to me."

There is a short pause, and then a voice from the back says, "I'll give $35."

An old gent who doesn't drive much in the city, goes to town and gets lost. He ends up going the wrong way down a one-way street. After several blocks he is stopped by a squad car. The police officer says, "You're going the wrong way." The old gent thinks about this a bit and then he slowly says, "How do you know where I'm going?"

A tourist stops at the local pub and orders a glass of beer. He drinks it down and questions the innkeeper: "If I could tell you how to sell 30% more beer, would you be interested?"
The innkeeper says, "I certainly would."
The tourist says, "Fill the glasses up."

You think that you've got problems.
My car won't start and the payments won't stop.

The only people who can honestly say that their problems are behind them are the school bus drivers.

I tried to save money by using less hot water, so I started to take cold showers. But, I got goose bumps so big, what I saved on hot water, I lost by wearing out the soap.

I used to work third shift in a zipper factory.
It was a real fly-by-night operation.

I was lucky to even get the job, considering I dozed off during the job interview.

Did you ever notice how long the days are when you get to work on time?

We all must believe in something. I believe I'll take a nap.

Yuk! This coffee tastes like Juan Valdez washed his socks in it.

A guy, answering questions for a life insurance application, is asked how much he weighs. He says, "I weigh 215 pounds with my glasses on." The agent asks him, "How much do you weigh with your glasses off?" The guy says, "I don't know. With my glasses off I can't see the scale."

From up in his bedroom a little guy calls out:
"I'm gonna say my prayers now. Does anybody want anything?"

Grandma thinks her grandkid is studying to be an astronaut because the teacher said he is taking up space in school.

When I was in school, I was a terrible speller...but my handwriting was so bad nobody knew.

I'll never forget the time I came home with four F's and a D on my report card. My dad said, "It appears that the kid is spending too much time on one subject."

One year I was voted poster child for Spring Fever.

I used to rob banks just to feel wanted.

My wife and I were very happy for many years. Then we met.

Her parents told her, "We don't mind you going out with a guy like him, but why a guy as much like him as he is?"

Our first really big fight happened the day of the wedding, right in the church, in the middle of the wedding ceremony. In those days the marriage vows included the "O" word: OBEY. When they asked: "Do you promise to love, honor and obey?" My wife said, "Do you think I'm crazy?" I was very nervous and without thinking I said, "I do."

I have no idea why she got so upset. I mean she certainly could've come with me on our honeymoon, but she had to work.

I asked why she wears her wedding ring on the wrong finger. She said, "Because I married the wrong guy."

She said, "I should have known you'd be hard to live with when the roaches moved out."

Talk about your pain and misery...my doctor told me that for two days I should drink plenty of water and stay in bed.

I've gone through three bottles of corn syrup and my feet still hurt.

Grandpa says, "Things have really changed. Now when you wake up sick at night, and call your doctor at home, he says, 'Take two aspirin and have your lawyer call me in the morning.'"

At 3 a.m. in the morning a guy gets a call from his neighbor who says, "Your dog is barking and I can't sleep." At 3 a.m. the next morning the guy calls the neighbor back and informs him, "I don't have a dog."

It's 2 o'clock in the morning. The phone rings and wakes her. She picks up the phone and hears her husband's voice saying, "Don't worry, honey, I'm safe."
She says, "Oh, I'm so relieved. Where are you?"
He says, "In jail."

I really pulled a boner this past Christmas. At the last possible minute I rushed out and bought 100 Christmas cards. They were on sale. Really cheap! So I didn't pay too much attention to the verse. I just addressed and mailed them. Then one day I read one of the few cards that were left over. Inside the verse read: "I'm sending you this card to say, a little gift is on the way."

A father to teenage daughter: "I want you home by eleven."
She says, "But, Dad, I'm not a child anymore."
He says, "I know...that's why I want you home by eleven."

Grandpa says, "In the old days it was the criminal, not the sentence, that was suspended.

Three friends are fishing when they notice the local warden walking towards them. One of the fishermen takes off running and is followed by the warden. After a considerable chase the warden catches the fisherman and asks to see his license. The fisherman reaches into his pocket and pulls out his license. The warden says, "If you've got a license, why did you run?" The fisherman says, "The other two guys don't."

The only reason I go to garage sales is to meet other people with no taste.

A mechanic puts a new bulb in a car's left rear turn signal and tells his new helper to go behind to see if it's working. The new helper goes behind the car and stands there looking at the car. The mechanic asks, "Are they working?" The helper says, "Yes...no...yes...no...yes..."

A guy sees a sign on the highway that says, "Last chance to buy gasoline at $1.05 per gallon." He pulls in and fills up. As he is paying the attendant, he asks, "How much a gallon is the gas down the road?" The attendant says, "$1.03."

First guy: "My wife and I argue a lot. She is very touchy. The least little thing sets her off."
Second guy: "You're lucky. My wife is a self starter."

Two people who work together meet outside a psychiatrist's office. The first asks, "Are you coming or going?"
The second says, "If I knew that, I wouldn't be here."

Many years ago in England a peasant was arrested and taken to court for calling the countess a pig. He questions the judge, "You mean I can't call the countess a pig?"

The judge says, "No you can't."
The guy then asks, "Is it okay to call a pig, a countess?"
The judge thinks about this and says, "Yes, that's okay."
The guy looks at the countess and says, "Hello, Countess."

A guy stopped me on the street in Detroit. He said, "Can you help me out? I don't have any money. I don't have any wallet. I don't have a watch. All I have in the world is this gun." I gave him my money, my wallet, my watch...

Over in England the police don't carry guns. Instead they carry whistles. I get this weird mental picture of them going after a criminal shouting: "Stop or I'll toot!"

One day, out of the clear blue sky, a boy walks into the house and confronts his parents with, "I hate this dull town. Nothing ever happens here. I want to go where there's action. I want to make some real money. I want to meet pretty women. I can't do any of that here so I'm leaving." Then he leaves. Before he gets to the street, his father calls to him from the window, but the boy doesn't listen. Instead he hollers back, "Don't try to stop me. My mind is made up!"
The father hollers, "I'm not trying to stop you. I wanna know if I can go along?"

Then there's the Chamber of Commerce fund raising committee that got things mixed up and had the local car dealership raffle off a church.

My neighbors have two lovely kids...and one ugly one.

The kid took second place in a "Beautiful Baby" contest. All the other kids tied for first.

A 4th grader had the sniffles and it annoyed the teacher so bad that she finally asked him, "Do you have a handkerchief?" He said, "Yea, but my mom won't let me loan it to anyone."

27

The hard-hat diver is walking on the bottom of the ocean when he gets a message from the ship: "Don't bother coming up; the ship is sinking."

It seems to me that most of the people who take all that "Assertiveness Training" are the very people who least need it.

Nurse: "Turn over. It's time for your shot."
Patient: "Does it make any difference which cheek you put it in?"
Nurse: "No...which cheek would you like me to put it in?"
Patient: "Yours."

I don't mind my kids having pets until the pets start having kids.

When I pass a barbershop, I like to just stop and reminisce.

Two guys are overheard talking on a street corner:
"I'm really feeling low."
"What's wrong?"
"Three weeks ago I found two hundred dollars."
"That makes you feel low?"
"Two weeks ago I won five hundred dollars in the lottery."
"That's terrible?"
"Then last week my rich uncle died and left me some money."
"So what's the problem?"
"This week, so far...nothing."

Foreman: "I wish you wouldn't make those noises when you work."
Employee: "I'm not working."

Boss to night watchman: "I wouldn't wake you up but this is important. You're fired."

Politicians are like ships. They're noisiest when in a fog.

Two drunks stagger onto a bridge and look down at the reflection of the moon in the water below. The following chat takes place:
"What's that?"

"That's the moon."
"...How'd we get way up here?"

How come the doctor's prescription isn't written as clearly as the bill?

I made a deal with my doctor. He said I can eat anything I want if I bring my account up to date.

I was in one really terrible restaurant. I mean it was really bad! Every Wednesday they run a special: $3.95 all you can stomach.

You know what they call Sushi in the South? Bait.

Trying to make a point, the attorney questioned the defendant: "You said that on the day in question you took the dog for a walk. Did you stop anywhere?"
The defendant says, "Did you ever take a dog for a walk?"

Passenger: "How high is this plane?"
Flight Attendant: "Thirty thousand feet."
Passenger: "Wow! How wide?"

Last month my wife found a blonde hair on my jacket, and she accused me of spending time with a blonde woman. Two weeks ago she found a red hair on my jacket, and she accused me of spending time with a red-headed woman. So lately I've been very careful to remove any hairs from my jacket. Now she's accused me of spending time with a bald woman.

I read where making new friends is supposed to improve your life. So last week I made two new friends. But my life didn't improve. Now I'm stuck with two new friends.

Overheard in the lunch room: "Tomorrow is Tuesday already...boy did this week go fast."

"Sorry, I don't kiss on the first date."
"How about the last?"

The boss said I'd get a raise when I earned it.
He's crazy if he thinks I'm gonna wait that long.

Officer: "Can you describe the person who assaulted you?"
Victim: "That's what I was doing when he hit me."

Anthropologists are very interested in the practices of those primitive tribes whose customs caused them to beat the ground with clubs while screaming loud, abusive cries of anger. They feel it may have somehow developed into the game of golf.

My brother-in-law quit his job to become a writer. He has even sold a few things. His car, his TV, his golf clubs...

One time he wrote and recorded a Country & Western song which led to the sale of quite a few record players in our home town. His wife sold hers. The neighbors sold theirs. I sold mine.

He sings in the key of "G," but it sure sounds like "L."

In his own way he has started paying me back the $10 he owes me. He borrowed $25 more, but only took $15.

A first grade teacher is grocery shopping and sees a man with a familiar face. She smiles and waves. The man gives a puzzled look and waves back. The teacher then realizes that the man is not who she thought he was. She attempts to explain with: "Oh, I'm sorry. I thought you were the father of one of my kids."

The experts seem to agree. If your parents didn't have children, most likely you won't either.

There are a lot of things I don't understand about opera. Like: When somebody gets stabbed, instead of bleeding, they sing.

She says her heart belongs to me, but the rest of her keeps going out with other guys.

My neighbor is a little weird. Last week, at 3 o'clock in the morning he was out in his yard with a flashlight trying to see if the sun was up yet.

What a guy! One time he took the first place trophy in a bowling tournament, but they found out about it so he had to give it back.

On a passenger cruise ship a woman falls overboard and is fighting to keep her head above water. For several seconds nobody offers to help her, but finally a 75-year old man goes over the railing and into the water. The woman clings to his body as he swims toward the ship. A life-boat is launched and the two are eventually returned safely onto the ship. That night a big party is thrown in honor of the old gent, who is a hero. He's the oldest man on the ship, yet only he came to the aid of the drowning woman. When they ask him to say a few words, he declines. Then they beg him to talk. Reluctantly he says, "I don't have anything to say, but I sure would like to know who pushed me."

I had an appointment, so I asked my wife to watch the boxing match and let me know who won. When I returned, I asked who won and she said, "Nobody won. One of the guys got hurt and they had to quit."

From a distance a small girl is showing some of her friends the bathroom scale. She says, "I don't know what it is, but when you stand on it, it makes you mad."

The gift that keeps on giving: A pregnant cat.

English guide: "This is where the Magna Charta was signed."
American tourist: "When was that?"

English guide: "Twelve, fifteen."
American tourist: "Let's go Martha, we missed it by 20 minutes."

Overheard in a meeting: "Please don't think of me as your boss. Think of me as your friend who is never wrong."

The only part of my car that doesn't make noise is the horn.

What a junker! Every time I stop, somebody reports an accident.

I now realize the value of having that heated de-fog type window on the rear hatch door. It keeps your hands warm when you push.

If they are really serious about making cars safer, they should forget about including a cigarette lighter.

Heard during a newlywed couple's first argument: "I don't know why you're so upset about my going out. I made that date long before we got married."

My attorney's new fee structure: he will answer three questions for $100. I confronted him with, "Isn't that a lot of money for just three questions?" He said, "Yes, it is. Next question."

Trying to make a good impression, I took some very important people to a great little restaurant I know of. The soup was great. The salad was outstanding. The steaks were magnificent. However, the pie was awful. The coffee couldn't have been worse. And I was double-charged for the after-dinner drinks. What a bummer. The place had changed hands right in the middle of our meal.

How come the Department of Agriculture keeps expanding while the number of farms and farmers keep declining?

Quite often it's easier to get forgiveness than to get permission.

Years ago my wife and I agreed our marriage should be a 50/50 proposition. Now I realize that I didn't know anything about women, and she didn't know anything about fractions.

At a family get-together I learned that my nephew is taking Nuclear Physics in college. I can't believe they'd let him do that. Milk of Magnesia should be strong enough for anyone.

"Honey, I can't get the car started. I think it's flooded."
"Let me try it. Where is it?"
"In the river."

You know what's a humbling experience? Whenever I would help the kids with their homework, their grades would go down.

I was standing in line at the car rental place in the airport. The woman in front of me was filling out a rental form, but paused for quite a while when it came to the part that asks your age. Finally the agent said, "The longer you wait the worse it gets."

In going over this month's bills I've had a big change of heart. That "buy then-pay now" plan isn't so great.

In an attempt to teach her class the value of money, the second grade teacher put several coins on the desk. Pointing to the first one she asked, "Does anyone know what this is?" One of the kids called out, "Heads."

An angry wife is berating her husband who is back in state prison. "Attempted robbery, attempted arson, attempted murder. Your record is absolutely shameful! You never succeed at anything."

Doctor: "Tell your wife not to worry about those symptoms; they're just an indication of advancing age."
Husband: "You tell her!"

Overheard at an Atlantic City hotel:
Guest: "When I made this reservation, I specifically requested a room facing the ocean."
Desk Clerk: "Well, you didn't specify which ocean."

"Waitress, I'll have the turtle soup...and make it snappy."

When I was a kid we lived in a tough neighborhood. Every morning when I was leaving for school, my mother gave me a dollar for the hold-up man.

I was reading about this television evangelist-type faith healer who actually made some guy walk. The evangelist was driving to the bank at the time and the guy was hitchhiking.

I asked my brother-in-law, "If someone gave you a million dollars, what's the first thing you would do?"
He said, "Count it to see if it's all there."

A while back he told me he kept dreaming about the number five. He said that even when he was awake, it seemed he would see the number five wherever he looked. He figured it was some kind of an omen, so on May 5th he went to the track and bet $500 on the fifth horse, in the fifth race. It came in fifth.

His doctor told him, "The best thing for you to do is to give up drinking, give up smoking and give up gambling."
He told the doctor, "I really don't think that I deserve the best...what's the second best.

Fact: 50% of doctors practicing in this country today graduated in the lower half of their class.

Overheard in court:
"Hey, judge, how ya doing, dude?"
"Fine one hundred dollars."

"I'm new around here. Who's the best lawyer in town?"
"That would be A.J. Schwartz, when he's sober."
"Who's the second best lawyer in town?"
"That would be A.J. Schwartz, when he's not sober."

A golfer swings his club, but misses the ball entirely. He looks at his partner and says, "Boy, this is a tough course."

"Waitress, I'll have a cheeseburger, some fries and coffee."
"Would you like to eat that here, or take it with you?"
"Both."

A politician is following a farmer around his farm talking about the upcoming election. Finally the politician asks the farmer, "Are you gonna vote for me?"
The farmer says, "You're my second choice."
The politician asks him, "Who is your first choice?"
The farmer says, "Who else is running?"

Daughter: "I told Tom you don't want him to see me anymore."
Father: "What did he do?"
Daughter: "He turned out the lights."

It's after midnight when the husband comes home.
The wife hollers out, "Is that you, honey?"
He says, "It better be."

Husband: "We haven't agreed on anything in six months."
Wife: "It's been seven months, dear."

"Some town. I've been to five stores and I can't get what I want."
"What do you want?"
"Credit."

Crash diet.
The first week I lost three inches from around my waist.
The second week I lost two inches from around my waist.
The third week I lost my pants.

"Okay, you say you're old enough...what'll you have."
"Brandy and wa-wa."

Daughter explaining about her new boyfriend to her parents:
"He's not a dropout. He was expelled."

Two young kids are watching a movie on television. The scene has a prisoner escape from prison and run for cover in a nearby woods. He is unable to contain himself and the kids hear him shouting, "I did it! I really did it! I'm free!"
One kid looks at the other and proudly proclaims, "I'm four."

Comedian Jeff Gengler was telling me that he was raised in a family that really believed "Laughter Is The Best Medicine."
He says, "Whenever I got sick, they'd just laugh at me."

New secretary to the boss: "I don't know why I always have to answer the phone. Most of the time it's for you."

Notice: The ESP Society will not be meeting this month due to unforeseen circumstances.

...and then there was the guy who took a cab to bankruptcy court and invited the cab driver in as a creditor.

A tenant complains to the landlord, "It's been raining for three days now and the roof leaks all over the house. How long is this going to go on?"
The landlord says, "What do I look like, the weather man?"

Father: "I think it's rather obvious that the kids get their intelligence from me."
Mother: "I can't argue with that. I still have mine."

A health nut is talking to his co-worker. The only thing he likes more than jogging is telling people about his jogging. He says, "I now jog to work behind the bus in which I used to ride to work. I feel great and I save $2.00 a day."

The friend says, "Why don't you save $20.00 and jog behind a cab?"

A woman with eight kids gets on a bus. The driver says, "Are all those kids yours, or is this some kind of picnic?"
The woman says, "They're all mine and it ain't no picnic."

You know what is embarrassing? Watching the boss do something that you just told him was impossible.

It was a night I'll never forget. We drove onto the beach. The moon was reflected in the water as I put my arms around her and leaned over to kiss her. My lips were trembling. Her lips were trembling. Our knees were shaking as we sat there lip to lip, shaking, quivering, trembling. Finally she looked at me and said, "Would you please turn off your stupid motorcycle?"

An old-timer who had never flown was taking out some insurance prior to a flight across Lake Michigan. On the application, one of the questions was: "Who should we notify in case of emergency?" The old gent put down: "The Coast Guard."

Correction to Trivia Quiz:
We regret last week's error in naming the stars of the 1954 movie THE HIGH AND THE MIGHTY. We have learned that Foster Brooks and Hulk Hogan weren't even in that movie.

A farmer calls his neighbor to find out what he did for his pig when it had distemper. The neighbor says, "I just gave it a pint of turpentine." The next day the farmer calls the neighbor back and says, "My pig died shortly after I gave it the turpentine." The neighbor says, "Yup...so'd mine."

BATH MAT: A little rug that wet children like to stand next to.

Following the presentation of evidence against a Kentucky moonshiner the judge asks the jury, "Do any of you have any questions that you would like to ask the defendant before you consider the evidence?"

After talking it over with the jury, the jury foreman stands up and says, "Yes, your honor, a couple of us would like to know how long he boils the malt and what is the best way to keep the yeast out?"

My wife left six pounds of Limburger cheese in the car overnight. Believe me, that's quite a phew!

I told her that our car now reminds me of that statue in Egypt. She said, "Sphinx?" I said, "Close enough."

The day we got married was the day our two worlds became one...and we've been fighting for the world championship ever since.

Some couples can't even agree before they get married. I heard one couple talking in the shopping mall. They couldn't agree on two rather picky little details for a wedding. She wanted the bridesmaids to wear long blue gowns, and he didn't want to get married.

A government official looking for equal rights abuses, interviews a company's personnel director. He asks, "How many employees does your firm have broken down by sex?" The personnel director says, "Five that I know of, but for us, theft is a much bigger problem."

Itemizing his personal belongings for his new insurance policy, the homeowner tells his agent, "This ax is an heirloom worth a bunch. It's been in my family for well over a hundred and fifty years."
The insurance agent says, "Really? It looks brand new."
The homeowner says, "That's because we take good care of it. Over the years it's had three new handles and two new heads."

A guy stopped me at the race track and wanted to know if I would give him a few dollars so he could get some food for his family. I said, "If I give you money, how do I know you aren't going to blow it on the horses?" He said, "No, I got money for the horses."

Jay Leno was approached by a mugger in New York City's Central Park. The mugger looked at him and said, "Hey, aren't you that comedian who's always on *The Tonight Show?*"

Somewhat relieved, Leno smiled and said, "Yes, I sure am."
The mugger said, "Put your hands up and don't try anything funny."

I spent a few days in a town where the locals were kinda strange. In particular I noticed they would play the horses, but instead of money they would bet with pebbles. A typical bet would involve some guy passing a few stones to the bookie, saying something like: "Put this on Danny's Pride to win." Then one day a guy came into town carrying a large boulder that he could hardly lift. As he approached the bookie, the guy next to me nudged me and whispered, "He must know something."

The local pub was a very rough place. All night long there was one fight after another. I felt it was probably safest for me to avoid making eye contact with anyone. Trying to be nonchalant, I said to the bartender, "That sawdust on the floor is like the old days." He said, "That's not sawdust; that's yesterday's furniture."

A young couple in a shopping mall: "If we skip two payments on the television, we'll have enough money for a down payment on a stereo."

A trio was making music for the residents of a nursing home. After the third song an old gent asked if they played requests.
The leader said, "Yes, we do. What would you like us to play?"
The old guy said, "Pinochle."

I joined an exclusive club for magicians called The Secret Six. This club is so secret, none of us knows who the other five are.

A woman was found guilty of poisoning her husband's coffee with a poison so powerful, a single drop would be more than enough to kill a bull elephant. Prior to sentencing her, the judge asked if at any time she felt any remorse. She said, "Yes, I guess I did." The judge asked, "At what point was that?" She said, "When he asked for a second cup."

A very rich, rather uppity woman was out with the new chauffeur on their first trip in her limo. She inquires, "What's your name?"
He says, "My name is Mike."

She says, "I prefer not to call the help by their first name. What is your last name?"

The driver says, "My last name is Darling."

After a moment of silence, she says, "Drive on, Mike."

One time my car rolled into another car while I was in the grocery store. The officer who took the accident report wasn't too smart . He asked me why I didn't think to use the car's emergency brake. I said, "What emergency? I just went in there to get a Twinkie."

I was visiting some friends and was telling them about my trip to Des Moines. I didn't realize how late it was getting until I heard the comment: "Maybe we should go to bed so you can go home."

I told them, "When the first rays of sunshine come through my bedroom window, I jump out of bed, ready to face another new day." What I didn't tell them is...my bedroom faces *west*.

Last week I was trying to fix the lawn mower. I was holding two parts in place, and I called to my wife to bring me a screwdriver. She yelled back, "We're all out of vodka."

A guy and his wife are sitting at the kitchen table answering the questions on a long application for an accident insurance policy.

She says, "It's asking here if you've ever had any accidents."

He says, "Nope. None that I can think of."

She says, "What about the time the neighbor's dog bit you?"

He says, "That wasn't no accident. He done it on purpose."

She: "Would you like to take a walk?"

He: "Yes, that would be nice."

She: "Don't let me stop you."

Two guys are talking. The first says, "I asked her to marry me, and she turned me down."

The other guy says, "Don't feel too bad. Often a woman's 'No' really means 'Yes.'"

The first guy says, "She didn't say 'No.' She said, 'Get lost'."

OVERHEARD IN A CHECK-OUT LINE AT THE MALL: That is the last blind date that I will ever go out on. He had a big honker of a nose and buck teeth. His nose looked like it was playing the piano.

This time they have gone too far. In an experiment involving the cross breeding of an abalone and a crocodile, scientists attempted to create an abadile. Unfortunately, something went horribly wrong and they ended up with a crockabalone.

Doctor to new mother: "It appears you're not getting enough sleep. If the baby starts to cry in the middle of the night, who gets up?"
She says, "The whole neighborhood."

IN A MARRIAGE COUNSELOR'S OFFICE: She says, "We were married by the Justice of the Peace. It should've been the Secretary of War."
...then he says,
"How many guys do you know who got slapped on their honeymoon?"
...then she says,
"When I don't praise him, he thinks I don't love him and when I do praise him, he thinks he's too good for me."

First guy: "I'm in trouble at home. My wife found a letter in my jacket that I forgot to mail."
Second guy: "You're lucky. Mine found one that I forgot to burn."

There is no truth to the rumor that the old saying: "Two heads are better than one" originated on a crowded Navy battle ship.

The photographers doing the *Sports Illustrated* swimsuit edition are on strike...for longer hours.

This week I'd planned to write a few comments about the importance of sticking with your decisions, but I've changed my mind.

While visiting my old Uncle Max, I suddenly realized I had eaten most of his jar of peanuts. I apologized but old Uncle Max said, "Go

41

ahead and eat 'em. Since I broke my upper plate, I had all I could do to suck the chocolate off."

Your perspective of the world is entirely different when you are only five years old and you are only three feet tall. Example: A mother and her young son were out shopping in the supermarket. In the laundry supply aisle they followed a very stout [that means fat] man who was pushing a shopping cart. The boy was obviously awed by the man's tremendous size and his mom was becoming worried that he'd embarrass her by saying something. In fact, she was so worried that she instructed the boy not to talk unless it was a real emergency. Just then a beeper on the man's belt went off, which was enough of an emergency for the kid. He grabbed his mother's arm and yelled, "Look out, he's backing up!"

Absolutely every mother has, at some time, used that great line: "Shut your mouth and eat." They must think you can put the food in through your nose. On the other hand, there were occasions when you'd get the giggles so bad the milk came OUT through your nose.

Now that I think about it, there's another great line mothers use. It's the old: "Are you kids asleep yet?" line. How the heck could anyone answer that one truthfully unless they talk in their sleep?

I used to wonder why my mother always sent me to bed when I wasn't tired, and then in the morning she made me get up when I was.

Once I would get to sleep at night, I could really sleep. And when she'd let me, I could sleep great in the morning too. But by the afternoon I'd just lay there tossing and turning.

One thing's for sure. I will never forgive my mother for spot-cleaning my face with spit on a handkerchief.

First guy: "What a fish! I caught a bullhead this long."
Second guy: "That's a lot of bull."

First guy: "I'm not kidding. I never saw such a fish."
Second guy: "Now *that* I believe."

I am happy to report that copies of the "Down Time" columns are being sent to our fighting men over at Murphy's Bar.

Talk about your unbelievable coincidences:
Every year I go on vacation at the very same time the fish do.

CONSUMER ALERT: At the top of the list of newly released products you should not buy are the new inflatable dart boards.

You know what I'd like to see? Just once, I would like to see a terrorist's letter bomb returned for insufficient postage.

And, one more time for those of you who still don't understand.
You CANNOT tell how old your telephone is by counting the rings.

And another thing...why should we be exploring outer space for intelligent life? If the life on other planets is so intelligent, we should save our money and let THEM discover us.

Maybe it just came out wrong, but one time I heard a politician who was running for office remark, "I have never done a dishonest thing in my life. All I want is a chance."

Some of our furniture goes back to Louie the 14th unless we can get some money to Louie by the thirteenth.

My parents always wanted me to become a surgeon but I couldn't stand the sight of money.

My mother used to talk to herself. Well, she thought I was listening.

With all the earthquakes in California lately I have to wonder why anyone would even want to live there? After the most recent quake, I asked a California friend of mine about it. I said, "Knowing you sit

right on top of the San Andreas fault and there are various other faults to worry about also, why do you want to live there?"
He said, "I love California in spite of its faults."

My brother-in-law must be mad at the phone company. He keeps knocking their poles down with his car.

He has more accidents than my neighbor's puppy.

Their puppy is finally paper trained. Now if they would only train it to wait until they're done reading the paper.

One night after many years of marriage, Grandma looks at Grandpa and says, "You used to snuggle a bit closer at night." So Grandpa snuggles a little closer. Then Grandma says, "You used to kiss me good night." So Grandpa kisses her goodnight. Then Grandma says, "You used to nibble on my ear." With that Grandpa jumps out of bed and runs down the hall. Grandma yells, "Where are you going?" Grandpa says, "To get my teeth"

My dentist keeps his prices down by keeping his overhead down. No unnecessary extras. Instead of laughing gas, he tickles you.

When you think about it, do we really need things like a spit sink? My dentist just changes his request to: "Rinse and swallow."

While traveling up the New England coast, I stopped for lunch at a seafood restaurant. The menu special was "Catch of the Day." That sounded good so I ordered it. About forty-five minutes later, when I still had not been served, I complained to the waitress. She said, "I'm sorry but so far today we didn't catch anything."

An employee of a rowboat rental operation stands on the shore of the lagoon with a megaphone calling: "Boat number ninety-one, it's time to come in now." When there is no response, he calls again: "Number ninety-one, your time is up. You will have to come in now." After a few more attempts with no response, he tells the manager. The manager informs him that they don't even have a boat number ninety-one. The employee thinks about this a bit and then calls: "Boat number sixteen, are you having trouble out there?"

They say: "A fool and his money are soon parted." Don't you have to wonder where the fool got the money in the first place?

You know what's a real bummer? When you send your picture to the lonely hearts club and they send it back with a note saying: "We're not that lonely."

OVERHEARD IN THE MESS HALL:
Lieutenant: "Soldier, do you have change for a dollar?"
Private: "I sure do, pal."
Lieutenant: "Not pal...I'm an officer! Let's try that again. Soldier, do you have change for a dollar?"
Private: "No, Sir."

Why didn't Noah kill both flies when he had the chance?

The company's delivery boy approaches the boss and asks, "Is it okay if I use the company car next Saturday?" The boss tells him, "Company policy normally doesn't permit using the company car for personal business. However, if you need it for something important, I may be able to make an exception." The delivery boy assures him, this is very important. "I'm going to get married next Saturday." The boss asks, "Well, who is the lucky girl?" The delivery boy says, "I don't know yet. I didn't want to ask anyone until I was sure that I could get the car."

COURTSHIP:
A time period when you try to determine if you can do any better.

The solitude of the neighborhood is shattered by a rowdy party in the big white house on the corner. The music is so loud it rattles the windows. Teenage kids in cars are coming and going everywhere. About that time a door-to-door salesman rings the front doorbell. The kid who answers the door has obviously been in a food fight.

The salesman says, "Is your mother home?"
The kids says, "What do you think?"

Here's a switch. My neighbor's kid got ticketed for going the wrong way on a TWO-WAY street.

My new sweater shrunk two inches and it was only partly cloudy.

I'm absolutely sure we bought one of those hide-a-beds a while back, but I'll be darned if I can find it.

A guy reports the theft of his wallet to the desk sergeant at the local police station. The next morning the desk sergeant calls him to tell him that they have four suspects in custody. The guy says, "I'm embarrassed to admit it, but I have made a horrible mistake. I found my wallet in my other pants. You can let the suspects go." The sergeant says, "We can't let them go. They've all confessed."

My brother-in-law was working part-time for awhile. Then he got fired....it was a full-time job.

I met my brother-in-law at the baseball game. He said he normally doesn't go to the ball game, but he was using his friend's ticket. I said, "Where is your friend?" He said, "He's probably home looking for his ticket."

As a kid in high school we used to practice baseball in the pasture out behind the school...until one day I slid into what I thought was third base.

I was always known as S.O.S. That's short for: Second Oldest Son. And sometimes they'd get confused and use: Second Oldest Brother.

Teacher: "There are three words that you seem to be using too much. They are: totally, awesome and righteous."
Student: "Wow! I'll try to lighten up. What are the three words?"

Psychiatrist: "This is your first visit so I need to know a little bit about you. Tell me about yourself, starting at the beginning."

Patient: "In the beginning I created heaven and earth..."

And then there was the psychiatrist who showed very poor taste when he equipped his waiting room with a cuckoo clock.

A guy finally gets up to the window after a long wait in line to get his license. He hears the ornery clerk briskly rattle off, "Spell your name, last name first, first name, middle name last."

The guy says, "What?"

The clerk scowls and repeats, "Spell your name, last name first, first name, middle name last."

The guy says, "O, double T, I, double U, E, double L, double I, double U, double O, a D, a Y, double A, one R, one O, and an N."

This time it's THE CLERK who's saying, "What?"

The guy starts over, "O, double T, I, double U, E, double..."

The clerk cuts him off and hollers, "Just say your name!"

The guy says, "Woody Aaron Ottiwell..the second."

I'm on THE MOUNTAIN CLIMBERS' DIET: I eat it 'cause it's there.

I also like THE NOAH DIET: Take two of everything.

OVERHEARD IN THE BANK:
"I hear you're looking for a new teller?"
"That's right."
"I thought you just hired a new teller?"
"That's the one we're looking for."

OVERHEARD AT THE LOCAL FISHING HOLE:
"Having any luck?"
"Pretty good..I haven't had a bite in two hours."
"What's so good about that?"
"The guys over there haven't had a bite in over three hours."

My wife and I pretty much like the same things. The difference between us is...I like to save it and she likes to spend it.

We get along very well. I don't try to run her life and I don't try to run mine.

A woman is telling her friend: "I just can't tolerate my husband's nasty disposition anymore. I'm so stressed I can't think straight. I have trouble sleeping, and I've lost my appetite to the point where I am losing weight. I am definitely going to leave him. However, I've decided I will stay until I lose ten more pounds."

There are three kinds of people in the world. Those who can count, and those who can't.

Preacher to congregation: "Can anyone tell me what we must first do before we can have a sin forgiven?" A guy in the back hollers, "Sin."

WIFE TO HUSBAND: "If you were a self-starter, I wouldn't be a crank."

"Do you know how to save a lawyer from drowning?"
"No."
"Good!"

The four basic food groups are: Meat, dairy, fruits and vegetables. And, just so you know...carrot cake is not considered a vegetable.

Speaking of vegetables...there is no way my brother-in-law's marriage can last...because she's a vegetarian and he's a meathead.

...One day opportunity did finally knock on my brother-in-law's door, but he was out buying lottery tickets.

SIGN IN THE WINDOW OF A DRY CLEANERS:
"We've been in the business since 1950...over forty years on the same spot."

They complain that the automobile is a polluter because of the problems it has with emission control. Well, correct me if I'm wrong, but I don't think horses were all that wonderful when it came to emission control.

My nephew told his parents that he is doing an experiment dealing with learning while you sleep. They, however, offer very little encouragement because he's doing the sleeping during class.

My doctor has ethics. He won't operate unless he really needs money.

A Frenchman explains the red, white and blue colors in the French flag to a guy from the U.S. "To us the flag symbolizes our taxes," he says. "We get red when we talk about our taxes, we turn white when we see our tax bill, and we are blue for months after we pay our taxes."

The U.S. taxpayer says, "I know what you mean. It's the same in the USA, only we see stars too."

STRIP POKER: The more you lose, the more you have to show for it.

No matter where Grandma hid Grandpa's booze, he somehow always found it. He had a kind of fifth sense.

A guy became totally obsessed with winning the lottery. He found himself thinking about it day and night. Before long he even began to pray that he would win the lottery. Soon it was the only thing that he prayed for. One day he dies and goes to heaven and he finds himself talking to God. He asks God, "How come my only prayer was never answered?" God says, "Well, for starters you should have at least tried to meet me halfway and bought a ticket."

OVERHEARD IN LUNCHROOM:
"How did your divorce come out?"
"The judge said we have to split everything fifty-fifty."
"How can you split the house fifty-fifty?"
"She gets the inside and I get the outside."

CHILDISH GAME: One at which your spouse beats you.

Two golfers are on the green waiting to putt when a ball comes flying through the air and lands about a yard from the cup. The first guy says, "Where did that come from?" The other guys says, "How should I know? Kick it into the hole." The first guy says, "Come on, we can't do that." The other guy says, "We can too. Whoever hit that ball violated all the rules of etiquette in the golf game. Kick the dumb ball into the hole." So they kick the ball into the cup.

Along comes the guy who hit it, several hundred feet ahead of his caddy. He says, "Did either of you guys see my ball?" They point to the cup. The guy goes over and looks in the cup. He starts muttering to himself, "I can't believe it. What a shot!" Then he turns and yells to his caddy, "On this hole I got a nine."

HOTEL DESK CLERK TO MAN AT THE COUNTER: "Somebody must have given you the wrong information...the Liars Club doesn't meet here."

POEM

She worried that time had taken its toll.
That her husband considered her charmless.
Then she looked at the crud, that once was her stud.
Now he's paunchy, all talk and quite harmless.

Our marriage ceremony has been bothering me. I contend that somewhere during the formalities I should have been allowed to make a phone call.

Q. What are your thumbs for?
A. To hold up the bottom of your hamburger.

"Waiter, I don't like all these flies buzzing around me."
"Point out the ones you don't like, and I'll see what I can do."

These days many churches will accept any and all denominations but mostly they prefer fives and tens.

OVERHEARD IN SUNDAY SCHOOL
Teacher: "Who was Moses's mother?"
Student: "She was the pharaoh's daughter."
Teacher: "Wrong. The pharaoh's daughter found Moses in the bulrushes."
Student: "Oh sure, that's what SHE says."

As a youngster in first grade I used to color pictures for my parents. Then one day they hid my crayons.

They used to send me to school; then they'd move.

I can't believe it. My neighbor just told me they're taking the word "gullible" out of the dictionary.

Labor Day traffic was bumper to bumper, so I turned the engine off and drove home in neutral.

Then coming through Iowa I heard a Des Moines radio announcer warn: "Drivers, if you are going north or south on I-80, be extremely cautious because I-80 runs east and west."

A state health inspector is investigating a local restaurant after getting complaints that they are using horse meat in their rabbit stew. After some questioning, the restaurant owner admits that there was some horse meat in the stew. "How much?" asks the inspector. The owner says, "We use about fifty-fifty." From the kitchen the cook yells out, "That's correct. It's fifty-fifty. One rabbit and one horse."

I bumped my head and sued. If they settle, I get a lump sum.

In school I was too nervous to play basketball. I lacked coordination. I'd be dribbling even when I didn't have the ball.

Q. Do you know why mountain climbers tie themselves together?
A. To keep the smart ones from going home.

A farmer who is known and liked by everyone in the county is accused of stealing a pig from a farmer who is not liked by anyone in the county. There is a jury trial and the jury quickly arrives at their verdict: "The defendant is found to be not guilty, but he has to return the pig." The judge tells them that there is too much of an inconsistency and they should try to reach another verdict. The jury goes back and is not heard from for a while. Then suddenly the door opens and they announce that they have reached a new verdict: "The defendant is not guilty and he can keep the pig."

A guy loses his wallet which contained fifty-five dollars. About a week later he gets the wallet back in the mail. It now contains forty dollars and an anonymous note that says: "A while ago I lost my wallet too...with fifteen dollars in it."

A politician was speaking to a large convention of interior decorators. When he was asked what his favorite color was, he said, "Plaid."

In the 1800's people avoided political speeches to the extent that a phenomenon known as "Gallows Politics" came into being. The politicians would show up at hangings where there was sure to be a crowd, and they would give their oratory there. But hangings usually took place early and the crowd wouldn't stay around for the speech.

The politicians then got the authorities to delay the hanging while they spoke, but with so many people on the platform, the crowd often was confused as to which one was the criminal. To resolve this problem it was decided that the criminals would stand there with the noose around their neck.

The problem now was the many complaints from those about to be hung. The courts agreed with the complaints and decreed that "An American had a basic right to be hung before rather than after a political speech." So prisoners were now given a choice as to when they wanted to be hung; before or after the politician's speech. The first offered this choice was a horse thief. When asked he thought it over for a while, and then wanted to know: "Who's speaking?"

Another criminal said, "Hanging is enough punishment. I'll go before!" One prisoner elected to be hung after the speech. Then, having listened to the speech, he thanked the politician for making it easier to die. Another prisoner who had decided to wait until after the speech, interrupted the windy speaker in the middle of his speech and suggested, "Don't you think the people have had enough?"

My favorite was the criminal who listened to the entire speech and then moved to the front of the gallows, with the noose still around his neck and delivered his own speech, which so moved the people that they were inspired to perpetuate his memory by electing him honorary mayor..."IN ABSENTIA."

OVERHEARD IN A HARDWARE STORE
"Do you have two, four-watt bulbs?"
"Two what?"
"No, four."
"Four what?"
"Yes."
"Could you come back tomorrow when the boss is in?"

TAXES
Supporting the government in the style to which it's become accustomed.

A third grader whose parents couldn't attend the annual school play, told them about it: "It was called Moby Dick," he said. "Some of the people saw it before, but they laughed anyway."

As a teenage boy starts the car to pick up his date, his father reminds him to drive carefully. The boy says, "You don't have to worry; we're going to be parked."

A woman puts an ad in the newspaper seeking someone to paint her house. The first guy to answer the ad says he wants $10 an hour to do the job. The second guy says he will do it for $8 an hour. So the woman hires the second guy and tells him he should start the first thing in the morning. Morning comes and the woman is very surprised to see both guys there. The first guy is painting and the second guy is just standing around giving various instructions. The woman says to the second guy, "What is going on here? I hired YOU to paint the house." The guy explains that he has subcontracted the first guy to do the painting. The woman says, "But he wants $10 an hour, and you're only getting $8 an hour. How can you make out?" The guy says, "I don't make out, but just once in my life I wanted to be the boss."

A guy and his wife are returning to their theater seats after going to the lobby for munchies. "Was that your foot that I stepped on when I left before?" he asks the man seated at the end of the row. "It was!" the man replies. The guy says to his wife, "Yup, this is our row."

A merchant calls one of his suppliers and places a rather large order.
The supplier says, "You have not paid us for your last two orders yet, so we can't ship this order until you pay for those."
The merchant says, "Well, cancel the order then. I can't wait that long."

My doctor told me that I really need to eliminate the stress in my life. He said I should have a hobby. In fact, he suggested I plant a garden. Now I'm really stressed. This summer I planted peas, corn and beans. Nothing came up...and I paid sixty-nine cents a can for that stuff!

Q. What, is an "O" turn?
A. That's when you start to make a "U" turn, and then change your mind

---

The warden was very upset that his daughter married one of the convicts. Partially because the guy was a lifer, but mostly because they eloped.

It takes two to argue, which is the same number it takes to get married.

The only thing my wife and I have in common is that we got married on the same day.

A guy I know told his wife-to-be, "Before we get married I want you to know I have had a few affairs with other women." She said, "Yes, I know, you told me last week." Then he said, "Well...that was last week."

TRIUMPH: Just a little oomph added to try.

It's his first night in the barracks, and at five-thirty the new recruit is awakened by the bugler playing reveille. He goes to the window and hollers, "You better go to bed; we've got a really big day tomorrow."

A guy goes to a newspaper office to place an ad offering $1,000 for the return of his wife's cat. "That's a lot of money for a cat," the clerk comments. "Not for this one," the guy says. "I drowned it."

A friend of mine cleaned out his junk drawer and found a claim ticket for a pair of shoes that he had left to be soled several years before. As a joke he took the ticket in and told the cobbler that he would like to pick up his shoes. The cobbler took the ticket into the back room. Several minutes later he came out and said, "They'll be ready Thursday."

Never lend money to a friend. It too often gives them amnesia.

...and then there was this guy who quit his job in California and looked for one in New York because he would get paid three hours earlier.

You know you're probably overweight when you put your old corduroys on and the ridges disappear.

Q. What do you get when you cross an elephant with a rhinoceros?
A. El-ef-I-no.

As a kid I went to a very rough school. We not only had a school nurse; we also had a school coroner.

Senior year there were two attempts to assassinate the class president.

The school didn't make us wear uniforms; we CHOSE to wear uniforms. Well...they weren't actually uniforms. They were flak jackets.

Speaking of jackets...my wife wants to go shopping WITH ME this year, just 'cause last year I bought two winter jackets at a two-for-one sale. What happened was I bought one...and then they sold me another one.

I readily admit it. I'm putty in the hands of anybody, selling anything. When I walk into a store, the boss calls back to the bookkeeper and says, "Go ahead and release the payroll...he's here."

I got a letter from the VISA people. It said I'm a credit to my card.

I overheard my wife talking to a neighbor lady. They both think I have that Clint Eastwood look...dirty and hairy.

My wife is mad again. I came home the other day and asked her what she was doing. She said, "I'm fixing dinner." And then, like a big dummy, I said, "I think it's beyond repair."

I am now making a conscious effort to get along with her. Every morning I now help her make breakfast. She makes the toast and I scrape it.

My doctor says I have to count calories. So far today I'm up to 9,430.

A little guy is acting up so his mom decides to put him down for a nap. The kid says, "How come every time you're tired, I have to take a nap?"

———

The only thing that kept me from going to college was high school.

———

One time I told my dad, "I made ten bucks playing poker and the teacher thinks I'm not doing very well." He said, "I think she means in school." I said, "This was in school."

———

Some childhood! My dad hired another kid to play me in our home movies.

———

A drunk and a priest are seated in a bus depot. The drunk decides to make conversation. "Parrrdn me, Father," he says, "but whatsa cause of arthritis?" The priest takes advantage of the situation and delivers a mini-sermon about the many evils of strong drink. He concludes with, "Arthritis could very likely be the result of indulging oneself with too much liquor." He then asks, "Son, are you suffering from arthritis?" The drunk says, "NO, but I was rrreading where the bishop is."

———

In Las Vegas a big-time gambler dies and a friend gives the eulogy: "Tony isn't dead. He only sleeps." A guy in the back of the room yells, "I got a hundred bucks that says he's dead."

———

A magician tells a reporter about the most difficult trick he ever did. "I once read a doctor's prescription written with a post office pen."

———

Don't mail your Christmas mail early this year or it could get mixed up with last year's.

———

CORRECTION: A typo in last week's column read: "My wife and I are married for twenty-six years now and she still looks like a newlywed." It should have read "...she still cooks like a newlywed."

———

Did you ever wonder if we all might still be in Paradise if Eve had tried to tempt Adam with broccoli?

———

My brother-in-law was known to everyone in town as "the town drunk."

And if that weren't bad enough, at the time he was living in New York.

At some point in time the North American continent tilted and everything loose rolled to the West Coast...and it's been that way ever since.

A motorcycle cop spotted a woman who was knitting while she was driving.

He pulled alongside her and shouted, "Pull over."

She shouted back, "No, it's a scarf."

Talk about your neurotic, frustrated pets...our pet turtle chases cars.

I made a deal with my wife. I will stop calling her "the little woman" if she will stop calling me "the big mistake."

Somehow I sent my utility payment to the IRS and my tax papers to the electric company. Now I just sit here in the dark and wait for a refund.

Last year, when daylight savings time ended, I realized that you cannot turn a digital watch backwards one hour to get back to standard time.

My wife said, "All you have to do is turn it ahead twenty-three hours."

I did...and for six months I was a day early for all my appointments.

Why always me? Yesterday I got a ticket for triple parking.

I try to mind my own business, but somehow I always get myself involved.

Like the other day...I was in the gas station when some woman was given a repair bill for her car. One look and she fainted right into my arms.

A crowd gathered and then someone yelled, "Stand back and give her air."

While I held her, the attendant gave her twenty-four pounds.

––––––

My doctor told me that he had some good news and some bad news for me.

I asked what the bad news was. He said that I'll need another operation.

I asked about the good news. He said that he won twenty bucks at bingo.

––––––

Minister: "Do you, John Larsen, take this woman for better or for worse, for rich or for poor, through sickness and in health, in good times and in bad..." The bride breaks in with: "You're gonna talk him out of it."

––––––

The president asked everyone to pray for the country, but not in school.

––––––

TWO LADIES ARE OVERHEARD AT THE FLOWER SHOW:
"The flowers are just beautiful, especially those asters."
"Those are chrysanthemums."
"Are you sure?"
"Yes, I'm sure! They're chrysanthemums."
"I'm going to write that down. How do you spell chrysanthemum?"
"Wait a minute...you're right...those are asters."

––––––

Our new coffee table was hand-carved...by the cat.

––––––

Pessimists think negatively. They think that times are so bad they can't get any worse. But I like to think positively. As bad as the times are, I'm positive they'll get worse.

––––––

A doctor gets a call from a woman who says, "My baby is starting to climb now and I'm afraid he might fall out of his crib onto the floor and I won't hear. What should I do?" The doctor says, "Remove the rug."

––––––

Two kinds of people easily fall prey to flattery. Men and women.

My wife is a mean cook. If she's mad at the kids, she gives them seconds.

LISP: That's when you call a spade a thpade.

These days we attack our personal problems differently. A good example:

Years ago a bed wetter would have gone to see a doctor with the problem. Now they go to a counselor who talks about self esteem, personal growth and loving yourself for what you are. After the costly sessions are over, the problem continues, but now you're proud of it.

Many senior citizens who can still vividly remember their first kiss have grandchildren who barely remember their first marriage.

TWO GUYS ARE TALKING OVER LUNCH: The first guy says, "My wife and I are very happy, but I often overhear her talking about her first husband."

The second guy says, "You're lucky. I keep hearing my wife talk about her next husband."

The wife is complaining to her husband, "You seem to know every single football statistic, but you can't remember our wedding anniversary or the year that we got married. He says, "I can too. It was the same year that the Packers traded Williams for a first round draft choice."

She says, "Don't you deny it. You love football more than you love me."

He says, "Well...I still love you more than basketball."

A father has just learned of his only daughter's plans to get married to some guy that she barely even knows. He asks, "Does he have any money?" She says, "Men are all alike...that's exactly what he asked about you."

I had heard that the traffic was really bad in the east, but I recently found out just how bad. Cars were backed up as far as I could see in every direction. Then some guy, several cars behind me, started yelling, "Please let me through. I have to deliver a very important message to President Ford."

The doctor says, "You've been very sick. For a while there I was afraid you weren't going to make it. I'm sure it was only your will to live that pulled you through." The patient says, "I hope you remember that when you send me the bill."

I am going to have a talk with the guy at my bank about the total lack of mutual trust. I mean, I am constantly giving them my money to use, with no questions asked, but every time I have to use one of their dumb twenty-nine cent pens, it's chained to the counter.

I guess my neighbor was checking to see if his tree died. The other day I noticed him out in the yard with the tips of his first two fingers on top of a branch and the tip of his thumb on the bottom of the branch, and he was looking at his watch.

Most often my doctor's prescription has to be taken to the drug store, but this time he said that I also had to take it to my travel agent. It was for a large bottle of Motrin and a trip to Lourdes.

THE MAGAZINE RENEWAL NOTICE READ: Dear Mr. Talbert. Please remit $19. Your subscription to *Sports Illustrious* magazine has expired.
HIS WIFE'S REPLY READ: Dear *Sports Illustrious*. So has Mr. Talbert.

At the annual Chamber of Commerce banquet the out-going president is commenting on the year that was. He remarks, "In nearly every chamber, half of the members do all of the work and the other half do nothing. Well, I'm happy to say that in our chamber it's just the opposite."

An out-of-work magician is once again trying to talk his landlord into waiting a week or so for the rent. He says, "Just think...in a few years tourists will pass this house and say, 'That's where The Great

61

Elmundo used to live.'" The landlord says, "If I don't get some money today, they'll be able to say that tomorrow."

I told a tourist, traveling here in Southwest Wisconsin, that this part of the state is known as "The Uplands" and that many of the rocks that you can see here today, were actually pushed here by the great glacier. He said, "Where is the glacier?" I said, "It went back for more rocks."

"Doc, what is wrong with me? I have dreams where I see talking dogs, talking mice, even talking ducks. Am I cracking up?"
The doctor says, "No...you're just having Disney Spells."

An employee is shorted five dollars on his pay check and he complains to his boss. The boss checks the records and confirms the error.
In checking the records, however, the boss uncovers additional errors. It turns out that the guy was paid ten dollars too much on each of the two previous checks.
The boss asks, "Why didn't you report those errors?"
The guy says, "Nobody minds a lousy mistake now and then, but this is three weeks in a row now."

Talk about errors. My horoscope said: "Yesterday's horoscope was wrong. Today is the day to invest your life savings."

...I invested everything I had on a company that makes elevator wigs for short bald guys.

What a flight! Over the PA we heard: "Because of a mechanical problem everyone will have to leave the airplane." So we all got off. But a mere five minutes later we were told to get back onto the plane.
As I walked past the flight attendant, I asked, "What's the problem?"
She said, "The captain discovered a bad leak in the flutter valve of the number two engine. He refused to fly the plane until they got a new flutter valve."
I said, "Did they get a new flutter valve?"
She said, "No, they got a new captain."

The guy who was sitting next to me must have been a first-time flyer. He nudged me and said, "Wow, the people look like ants." I said, "Those are ants. We haven't taken off yet."

When they told everyone to put their seat into a upright position prior to take-off, he tried to do a head-stand.

My brother-in-law is with the FBI. They caught him last week.

There was a new drink that came out this fall. It's called: "The Autumn Cocktail."
After drinking two, you turn colors and fall to the ground.

Did you ever notice, whenever you hear the word "save" on television, it's part of some commercial that's designed to get you to spend?

I'm at that age where if I go all out, I end up all in.

I was cleaning out the attic the other day and I came across some love letters that my wife had saved. They were dated last week.

She's a big Billy Joel fan. I asked her what he has that I don't have. She got laryngitis telling me.

My psychiatrist told me that she probably doesn't mean those things. He said I have a persecution complex. That's what I expected he'd say. The guy hates me.

OVERHEARD IN THE BARBER SHOP: "We are plagued with too much government. On the other hand, if you think we're getting too much government now, can you imagine what it would be like if we got all we're paying for?"

The government gets a very large chunk of every check we take home. Knowing this, and knowing the state of the U.S. budget, I feel that my brother-in-law should feel extra guilty when he misses a day of work, because the government is losing almost as much as he is.

What I like most about him is, I never get the feeling that he knows something I don't.

Last week he decided to improve his personal image, so he went out and bought a toupee. It makes him look ten years stupider.

He was telling me that he almost shot an elk up in northern Wisconsin. "I doubt it was an elk," I said, "because Wisconsin has no elk."
He said, "Well, this guy was. He had a membership card in his wallet."

The Boy Scouts have been advised not to purchase the Tates compass because they don't work. In fact they're the basis for the old saying, "He who has a Tates is lost."

Some of the "old sayings" are anything but good advice. For example, you'll notice that the fire department doesn't fight fire with fire.

Certainly birds of a feather flock together. How else can they flock?

Speaking of a fool and his money, my brother-in-law's monthly payments were getting to be way too much for him, so he consolidated all of his monthly obligations. Now there's only one bill that he's not paying.

Last week he got stopped by the state patrol for exceeding the 50 m.p.h. speed limit. He told the officer, "It said sixty on the highway sign."
The officer said, "Sixty is the highway number, not the speed limit."
From the back seat his kid said, "You should have seen him on I-90."

One easy way to get your family tree traced is to run for office.

And then there was the candidate who refused to answer some tough questions on the grounds that they might eliminate him.

The neighbor couple just had a big fight, but now she is trying to smooth things over. At least I think she wants to smooth things over. She went after him with an iron.

It's absolutely not true that women have trouble keeping a secret. They can keep a secret. It just takes more of them to do it.

This Thanksgiving I was very thankful. Mostly I was thankful that things aren't as tough for me as they were when I was a kid growing up. We were poor. When the need would arise, mother used to take in wash off other people's lines.

I remember one year we were invited to Grandma's house for dinner.
Grandpa said, "This turkey tastes funny. What did you stuff it with?"
Grandma said, "I didn't have to stuff it. It wasn't hollow."

I hated to travel anywhere for Thanksgiving because I used to get so car sick. Then one time my mother got some stuff called Dramamesia This stuff was kind of a combination of Dramamine and Milk of Magnesia. I didn't get car sick, but we still had to stop quite often.

A couple drives for hours and hours, trying to escape that rat-race of the big city. They drive down back roads and narrow country lanes until they end up in a very small town that is miles and miles from anywhere. They stop and get out of their car, wanting to take in the peacefulness of the place. In the local general store they comment to the owner, "Everything in the country is so nice and quiet. Life in the country is so much better than the crazy pace of life in the city. Don't you agree?"
The owner says, "I can't rightly say. I've never lived in the country. I've always lived right here in town."

One old timer was telling me that years ago they tried to put a 10 p.m. curfew into effect here in Dodgeville. I guess it lasted just a few days and then they had to stop because they got so many complaints.

He said, "Every night at 10, the whistle would go off and wake everyone up."

A purse snatcher is arrested and insists on acting as his own lawyer. When he cross-examines the victim he asks, "Did you get a good look at my face when I took your purse?"

My neighbor told me his girlfriend is a twin.
I asked him if he ever kissed the wrong twin.
He said, "No, her brother won't even come near me."

I didn't mind my hair starting to turn grey, but now it's turning loose.

A lot of people think that jogging is something new. It really isn't. My great, great grandfather was already jogging back in Civil War days. Back then they didn't call it jogging. When they finally caught him, they called it desertion.

They're getting a bit tougher in the courts lately. I was just reading about a judge who gave some guy three months of solitary confinement and two months in the electric chair.

Patient: "I told the pharmacist about my symptoms."
Doctor: "I'd be interested to know what foolish advice he gave you?"
Patient: "He told me to see you."

Father to daughter: "Until you are a bit older, if you want to date, you will have to double date."
Daughter to father: "That's okay with me."
The following Saturday night two boys stopped over to take her out.

Little girl to mom: "I want a baby sister for Christmas."
Mom to little girl: "There aren't enough shopping days left."

I would have been a very rich man today, but several years ago I invested everything I had in a chain of slow-food restaurants.

I was on a flight that was extremely bumpy. The guy next to me wasn't taking it well. When the meal was served, he told the flight attendant, "Let's save an entire step. Put mine directly into my sick-sack."

Lesson #3, Understanding and Using Prefixes:
The prefix PRO and the Prefix CON give opposite meanings to a word.
Example: Progress/Congress.

Wife to husband with a hangover:
"How can your head hurt this morning? You sure didn't use it last night."

Question: What normally follows two days of rain?
Answer: Monday.

The judge says to the plaintiff, "Explain what happened."
The plaintiff says, "I was in a phone booth talking to my girlfriend when the defendant opened the door and dragged me out."
The defendant says, "The only reason I dragged him out is because he refused to get out, and I needed to make a phone call."
The judge asks, "How long were you talking to your girlfriend?"
The plaintiff says, "I don't know, your honor, but I want to add that he dragged my girlfriend out too."

The bailiff says, "All rise." My attorney says, "I object."

CRUEL AND UNUSUAL PUNISHMENT:
The warden slips a whoopee cushion onto the electric chair.

My brother-in-law says he is a model salesman. That may be true, but he isn't a working model.

I'll never forget the year he got his wife a mood ring for Christmas. No matter what mood she was in, it turned her finger green.

A woman says to her husband. "We're married for twenty-two years now. Every night we do the same old stuff. Just once, why don't we go out and really live it up?"

Speaking softly, so as not to be heard by the little old lady who is rocking in the front room, the husband says, "Okay, but can't we leave your mother home this time?"

The wife says, "My mother! I thought she was your mother."

Lately it seems like I don't have to worry about avoiding temptation. At my age temptation is avoiding me.

OVERHEARD IN A SINGLE'S BAR:
"Mark, this is Joe. Joe, this is good-bye."

My wife has made it very clear to our dog that there are inside toys and there are outside toys. When the dog tries to bring a stick into the house, my wife stops her with a sharp, "No, no! Sticks are for outside." Two weeks ago the dog gave me a: "Boy you're gonna be in trouble!" look when in through the front door I dragged our Christmas tree.

A psychiatrist is a person who tries to find out what's kooking.

It is widely accepted that you're more likely to retain the knowledge gained by doing something wrong, than that gained doing something right. In that case, somewhere, my brother-in-law must have tons of knowledge.

He told me that at night when he is trying to sleep he sees shadows all over his bedroom. I asked him if he has ever seen a psychiatrist. He said, "No. Just shadows."

Anyone who goes to a psychiatrist should have their head examined.

SOMETIMES YOU CAN MISINFORM EVEN WHEN YOU TELL
THE TRUTH

A lesser known presidential candidate gave a speech in a small town. Within the speech he used various jokes to brighten up the message.

After the speech he met with the members of the local press and said, "Please feel free to quote me, but please don't print the jokes I told, as I would like to use them in future campaign speeches."

The next day the paper carried the headline: "Candidate tells several jokes which we can't print."

I was reading somewhere that the odds of getting onto a plane that has a bomb on it are about a million to one. However, the same mathematician claimed that the odds of getting onto a plane that has two bombs on it are ten million to one. So I figure, whenever I fly, I'll carry a bomb.

Back in ancient times a brilliant mathematician came up with the concept of Zero. Prior to that there were positive and negative numbers but zero hadn't been used. Knowing that the zero was an important new concept, a dinner was given in honor of the scholar. A banner behind the head table read: "Thanks for nothing."

I had a car accident and I have to go to court. To make matters worse, I may have weakened my case when I filled out the dumb accident report. I accidentally signed my name on the line that asks, "What was the probable cause of this accident?"

He: "If I could do it all over again, do you know who I'd marry?"
She: "Who would you marry?"
He: "I'd marry you."
She: "That's what you think."

She says: "Why can't you be a bit more like our neighbor. He takes his wife out to dinner. He takes her out dancing. He takes her to the show. Why don't you ever do that?"
He says: "I would...but I don't think he'd let her go."

A guy is complaining to his friend: "You see, the reason I can never win an argument with my wife is because I can't get a word in edge-wise. When I start to say something, she starts in again, and there I stand with my mouth open. Then I'm in trouble 'cause she thinks I'm yawning. I'm gonna start calling the dog 'Sweetie' and her 'Old Yeller.'"

The new teller is overheard counting packages of singles in the bank: "...54, 55, 56." Then he throws the entire package back into the drawer. He mumbles, "If it's right that far, it's probably right all the way."

A guy is getting a haircut in a small town barbershop when the fire siren goes off. He jumps out of the chair and says, "I've gotta go."
The barber says, "What for? You're not on the fire department."
The guy says, "I know...but my girlfriend's husband is."

I told my neighbor that when I drink coffee I can't sleep. He told me that he is just the opposite. When he sleeps, he can't drink coffee.

He drinks liquor. He says that it relaxes his nerves. Several times I've seen him so relaxed he couldn't move.

Christmas Eve he hung his stockings up and the poinsettia plant died.

He's nobody's fool. On the other hand, maybe someone will adopt him.

A while back I was on a farm and noticed that the farmer was carrying his pigs down to the stream, one by one. He said that he was taking them down for a drink of water. I said, "Wouldn't it save time if you brought some water up to the pigs?" He said, "What is time to a pig?"

Question: What do you call a boomerang that doesn't come back?
Answer: A stick.

Six guys walk into a restaurant and are seated at a table. The leader goes over to the manager and says, "These people are patients from the Walker County Institution. This is our weekly outing. They will probably try to pay you with bottle caps. This is okay. Accept the bottle caps. It's part of the recovery program. When they go back to the bus, I will settle up with you."
The manager agrees to go along with this, so they all order and eat. They pay for their dinner with bottle caps and get back onto their bus.

As the leader walks over to the cash register the manager tells him, "The bill comes to ninety-six dollars and forty-two cents."
The leader says, "Do you have change for a hubcap?"

Remember: It's okay to let a smile be your umbrella, but if you do, it's bad luck to open your mouth in the house.

My brother-in-law is off work for a while. He got hurt on the job. Nothing serious, but he is bandaged, very stiff and he can hardly walk. As I understand it...

He was hired to remove some bricks from the roof of a big old building. I guess he was on the ground holding the end of a rope, and he had the rope strung through this pulley affair up on the roof. On the other end of the rope, up on the roof, was a big wheelbarrow. He had loaded the wheelbarrow with bricks, and his plan was to lower it down with the rope.

Turns out that the wheelbarrow was heavier than him and the thing came down hard and fast, pulling him swiftly upward. In fact, he was yanked so hard that he sprained his wrists and nearly dislocated both shoulders.

Halfway up, he met the wheelbarrow coming down, and received a nasty bump on his head and numerous cuts and bruises to his arms and his back. As the wheelbarrow went down, he continued up.

At the top he met the pulley rather abruptly, causing injury to his fingers and knuckles and giving him some wicked rope burns on the palms of his hands. Meanwhile, on the ground, the wheelbarrow stopped suddenly and spilled all the bricks. So now he is heavier than the wheelbarrow, and he comes speeding downward and the wheelbarrow goes speeding upward.

As you can imagine, halfway down he meets that dumb wheelbarrow again, but this time the thing is going up, and it inflicts damage to his shins and catches him smartly under the chin. He continues down and hits the ground with such force that he sprains an ankle and throws his back out. He said that he can vividly remember thinking, "Thank God, that's over!" But it wasn't. He made the foolish mistake of letting go of the rope.

He said, "I look up, and here comes that stupid wheelbarrow again..."

. He does the work of three men. [Larry, Curley and Moe.]

What a guy! He thinks Abraham Lincoln is a Jewish car dealership.

Why is everyone named Bertha, fat?

And then there was the science teacher whose experiment exploded and blew him ten feet into the air. He said, "I guess I should have been more specific when I prayed for a raise."

Last week, when my wife and I went out for dinner, I could tell she was mad about something. Through the entire meal there was total silence...except for the celery.

The neighbors seem to have the perfect marriage. He'd rather play golf than eat...and she'd rather go to auctions than cook.

They are really addicted. In his sleep he often hollers out, "Fore," and she answers, "Four-fifty."

He bought a brand new mini van with that wood paneling on the sides. A couple of days later when I saw it, the thing looked like he had been in some kind of accident with it.
He said, "That's the way it looked when I took it out of the crate."

The owner of a corner tavern gets an early morning call at his home from some guy who wants to know what time his tavern is going to open. The owner says, "I get there at 10 a.m., and I open at 11 a.m."
An hour later the guy calls again and asks what time the bar opens. The owner says, "We open at 11 a.m."
About twenty minutes later the same guy calls for a third time and asks what time the bar is going to open. The owner says, "I told you, you can't get in until 11 a.m."
The guy says, "I don't wanna get in. I wanna get out."

Socialized Medicine: When people mingle and talk about their operations.

A MOTORIST IS STOPPED BY THE STATE PATROL:
The officer says, "I clocked you going seventy miles an hour."

The motorist says, "No way...I've only been driving for ten minutes."

An out-spoken, elderly woman is being examined for possible jury duty. The defense attorney asks if she might know the plaintiff's attorney. She says, "Yes, he's a no-good crook."
The plaintiff's attorney then asks if she knows the defense attorney. She says, "I do, and he's a no-good crook too."
The judge calls the two lawyers to the bench and says, "If you two know what's good for you, you better not ask her if she knows me!"

There is truth in advertising. I saw that junker car I used to drive. It's on the dealer's lot, and it has a great big sign on it that reads: "TODAY ONLY - $499 - THIS ONE WON'T LAST LONG."

It's some kind of unwritten law that drivers under 30 drive over 70 and drivers over 70 drive under 30.

Health care is getting far too expensive. I just got a prescription. The instructions read: "Take one every time you can afford it."

I was in line at the store behind a farmer who was buying rat poison. The clerk asked if he'd like it in a bag to carry home. The farmer said, "I suppose...unless you can get the rats to come down here to eat it."

USELESS INFORMATION: The words CHOICE COD read the same when held upside down in front of a mirror.

Talk about reading...my neighbor is reading a book. He says that the plot takes a strange twist. It's about a Frenchman who is disappointed in love, so he joins the American Legion.

The reason he finds it interesting is the story is very similar to an experience his uncle had during World War I. His uncle was jilted by a woman who was later mentioned three times in one of the most famous military songs ever written. TRAMP, TRAMP, TRAMP, THE BOYS ARE MARCHING.

POEM [anonymous]

Weep and they'll call you a baby.
Laugh and they'll call you a fool.
Yield and they'll call you a coward.
Stand and they'll call you a mule.

Win and they'll say that you cheated.
Lose and they'll say you don't try.
You're damned if you do, you're damned if you don't.
That's life 'til the day that you die.

Shortly after mentioning that we got married in '65, my friend Bob told me that 65 Kennedy half dollars are worth $32.50. Later he added that 66 of them are worth $33.00.

But enough about Kennedy. February is the month we salute Washington. First in war, first in peace, and they won the Super Bowl too.

I'll say this much about George Washington. He never once blamed his problems on the previous administration.

Last February my wife and I spontaneously decided to drop everything and go to Las Vegas. To get money for gambling we took the funds from our IRA retirement fund. I can now confirm, first-hand, there really is a substantial penalty for early withdrawal. I don't know what they do at other banks, but the guys at my bank dragged me into the back room and slapped me around.

As we drove to the airport we were very excited about our vacation. We would be SPENDING the next four days and three nights in Las Vegas. I jokingly asked my wife if she remembered to pack her swimming suit.
She said, "Yes, I packed my swimming suit, but I wish I would have packed my heavy coat."
I said, "We're going to Las Vegas. Why do you need your heavy coat?"
She said, "The plane tickets are in it."

A sign at our hotel gave the hours that meals were served. It read: "Breakfast is served from six to ten. Lunch is served from ten to four.

Dinner is served from four to eight." My initial response to this was: "That sure doesn't leave much time for anything else."

By the second day we were already fighting. It wasn't my fault either. It all started when I decided to take a nap while she played the slots. When she returned, she said, "If I tell you how I blew $400, will you promise not to laugh?"

OVERHEARD IN A RESTAURANT:
"Don't turn around but who is that who just walked in?"

I found out the hard way that when you are at an auction, you can get something for nodding.

I ended up buying this 1978 car that had chrome on all four fenders. It had chrome all over the hood. It had chrome all over the dashboard. Chrome everywhere. It was absolutely the chromiest car I've ever seen.

When my daughter was sixteen, I bought her a car. It was the only way I could get to use the phone.

On TV awhile back, I saw an ad for some of that powdered diet stuff, so I decided to try some. I didn't lose any weight, but I will say that it tastes pretty good sprinkled on a banana split.

You've got to wonder if anyone proofreads those ads on television. Last night I saw this laxative ad where the main selling point was that the stuff works while you sleep. That doesn't sound too wonderful to me.

Well, as long as I've already sunk to that "no class" brand of humor, I'll briefly mention the time I drank 8 Cokes and burped 7 up.

I've been dealing with my bank for weeks now, and they are finally going to give me a five percent loan. One problem, however. I found out that it's five percent of what I wanted.

My neighbor applied for a job where security was extremely important. They said that they were looking for a guy who knows how to keep his mouth shut. He told them that he could keep his mouth shut. They said, "Okay, we'll see," and they started him out at less than minimum wage.

This month I turned fifty-one and after all these years I've finally made up my mind what I want to be. I want to be twenty-one.

These days you've got to watch out for yourself. There are those misleading 900 telephone numbers and the phony contests in the mail. You have to see through the sophisticated contracts and sales pitches. There was a time this country had more whittlers and fewer chiselers.

Everything is changing. My travel agent says that women and children no longer go first into the life boats if there's an emergency at sea. The cruise lines have a new policy which states that the first to get the life boats are those on the "Go now - pay later" plan.

I was looking over my income tax forms. The IRS has page after page of the various schedules. What I need is a schedule of loopholes.

Now the tax preparation people are starting to think like the IRS. Soon TV ads will say, "REASON #147 WHY H&R BLOCK SHOULD DO YOUR TAXES. To find reason #147, subtract reason #94 from reason #123, unless you have answered 'yes' to reason #16 and your number of dependents is equal to or greater than the lesser of reason #8 and #31, if filing jointly."

I just found out that my neighbor got a raise. His annual income went from $25,000 to $28,000 a year, but he can't brag about it to anyone, because everyone already thinks he's making $50,000.

Nobody in town knew who he was. So to make an impression, he went out and bought a brand new car. Now when he drives around town, people say, "There goes what's-his-name."

76

Last week I saw him out in his garage. He had his wife's ironing board and was trying to make a six-man skateboard for the kids.

A sign on the garage behind the small church reads: "NO TRESPASSING," and in small letters is the following: "but if you do, you're forgiven."

The trouble with the economy today is everybody's buying stuff on time, but nobody is paying for it on time.

My wife keeps saying, "It's the thought, not the money. When I met you, I thought you had money."

My doctor said I have too much stress in my life and I should try to take my problems one at a time. I said, "I can't get them to line up!"

The wife says: "The older Mary gets, the more HER husband loves her."
The husband says, "Well, certainly. He's an archaeologist."

Little Johnny's parents to his teacher: "We're not complaining but we can't believe that you gave him another 'A' in English. He can't spell. He's constantly misusing words. And his sentence structure is terrible. The teacher says: "Well, I think he done good."

My daughter said, "I wonder what I should do with my old clothes?" I said, "Why don't you try wearing them?"

POEM
[Anonymous]
Her cookie jar is always filled.
Her car is at the ready.
She never yells when milk is spilled.
She lets her kids go steady.
She even lets them stay out late.
Takes their side when they fight with another.
Who is this woman who sounds so great.?
It's everyone else's mother.

77

My brother-in-law has been evicted so many times he decided to buy drapes that match the sidewalk.

What a restaurant! The chef was very consistent. The wine, the salad, the steak and the coffee were all the same temperature.

In my opinion all the corporations should have regular fire drills. Then employees will know what to do when they get fired.

President Clinton tells his limousine driver that he has always wanted to drive a limo. The limousine driver says, "Why don't we switch places and you can take the wheel." So they switch. Unfortunately, the President gets carried away and he is stopped for speeding. The officer looks at who is driving and he goes back to his squad car to call into headquarters. The officer says, "I'm involved in something REALLY BIG. I don't know who I stopped. But Bill Clinton is his chauffeur."

Everything is messed up. Why don't they just send the best produce to the supermarket instead of the county fair?

If I had any more kids, I wouldn't send them to college. I'd just give them the money and let them retire.

In an economics class the professor wanted someone to name anything where the supply exceeds demand. A kid in the back says, "Trouble."

I'll never again travel with my brother-in-law. He called the hotel's front desk to complain that he couldn't get out of his room. He said, "One door leads into the bathroom. One door leads into the closet. And the third has a sign that says, 'Do not disturb.'"

Television is a great teaching tool. The neighbor kid is only six, and he watches so much TV that he is already an expert on body odors.

I asked the kid what he'll do when he is big like me. He said, "Diet."

The one subject I will not joke about in this column is MY sex life. What was, was.

Good record keeping is an important part of running the government. For example, Congress uses a bookkeeping system that involves a very elaborate system of checks and bounces.

I'm glad they blew the whistle on Congress's check writing habits. However, now I worry that the country will go broke buying whistles.

My brother-in-law should be in Congress. He even thinks like they do. He figures if he gets to work late and leaves work early, he will make fewer mistakes.

Here's a beauty. One time we were in a boat fishing and he accidentally dropped his watch overboard. As we watched it sink out of sight, he said, "Don't worry; it's waterproof."

You know what is no fun at all? When you are driving through the worst section of a big city, behind a bunch of guys from a motorcycle gang, and you accidentally lean on your horn.

I wish I had half as much fun when I travel as my wife thinks I do.

Every year my wife throws a big party on our anniversary, but she never tells me where.

The local Slender Center place gets some really strange telephone calls. One woman called and said, "I want to lose some weight so I can get into the birthday present I got from my husband."
They told her, "Don't worry. We'll have you in that dress in no time."
She said, "It's not a dress. It's a Geo Metro."

A guy I went to high school with tried out for Major League baseball. He was a great shortstop, and he had a .345 batting average. But he didn't make it because he wasn't arrogant enough.

Dear Ted. Can you ever forgive me? I now realize that you are the only one I ever really loved. I should never have treated you the way I did. It's not that I wanted to avoid you. It's just taken me this long to get my life in order and establish my priorities. Please call me real soon. I would really love to hear from you again. We have a lot going for us. Until then, I want you to know that I'll always love you. Signed, Linda. P.S. Congratulations on winning the state lottery.

My neighbor drove quite a distance to get to a certain movie theater last Monday night. When he got there, it was closed. I guess he didn't understand their sign which read: "Good, clean family entertainment every night except Monday."

And then there was the street cleaner who was fired because he couldn't keep his mind in the gutter.

OVERHEARD IN RESTAURANT
"Today was the day everyone in the plant took that honesty test."
"How did you do?"
"Well, put it this way. It's a good thing I own the place."

At our house I pretty much say anything I like. My wife accepts it. Where I get into trouble is mentioning those things I don't like.

She must have been very nervous about doing things in the proper order during our wedding ceremony. Over the years several people have told me that, as she approached the front of the church, they clearly heard her mumble, "Aisle, Altar, Hymn."

I have to lose weight. My doctor said the best way to lose weight is to drink warm water an hour before every meal. Well, I just can't do it. I'm okay at first, but after about ten minutes of drinking I feel bloated and sick.

OVERHEARD IN THE RECEPTION LINE AT A POLITICAL FUND RAISER

"You probably don't even remember me from back in the days when you first ran for public office. If you recall, I made your banners."

"Certainly I remember. It's so nice to see you again, Major Banners."

Dinner guest: "We hate to eat and run but we're still hungry."

She asks him to come to her home for dinner and to meet her parents. For a while he makes a fairly good impression, but then her father asks, "Do you have any objection to having a martini?"

He says, "I've never had one before."

Her father says, "You've never had a martini before?"

He says, "No, I've never had any objection to having one."

CHARLES DICKENS MARTINI: No olive or twist.

Reviewing the proper use of the verbs "setting" and "sitting," the teacher asks one of the boys to use the word "setting" in a sentence. The boy says, "The cat was setting in our yard."

The teacher then reminds him that those things that have life "sit," and those things that don't have life "set."

The boy comes back with, "The dead cat was setting in our yard."

NEIGHBOR TO NEIGHBOR: "Our puppy is weaned. He's eating solids now: shoes, furniture, the broom handle..."

I like small towns. Small towns are usually friendly. That's good. But sometimes it can go too far. Like the other day, I was taking a shower when I heard my neighbor knocking on the shower curtain.

He comes over to tell me about his problems. He said that when he had his new furnace installed the salesman told him it would pay for itself, but every month they still send him a bill.

This year in America "Spring House Cleaning" will take place during the fall, and my guess is that we will clean out the Senate too.

While most of us feel that both the House and the Senate are loaded with problems, there are those who say that they only have one problem. They can't do anything right.

At a city council meeting, called to discuss the recent problems with video poker machines in some of the local taverns, someone suggested: "We don't need a law banning video poker machines. We already have one banning the use of mechanical traps used to catch dumb animals."

I called for an appointment with the doctor. I was told that they couldn't fit me in for at least two weeks.
I said, "I could be dead by then."
They said, "That's no problem. Just have your wife let us know, and we will cancel the appointment."

A guy telephones his lawyer to go over the bill that the lawyer sent. He says, "We got together for a few rounds of golf and we had lunch. What's this $25 charge for counseling and advice?"
The lawyer says, "Don't you remember? I told you to keep your head down and I recommended the beef tips."

Q: How many teamsters does it take to change a light bulb?
A: Seven. You got a problem with that?

An English teacher calls the National Broadcasters Association office to complain. She says, "I cannot believe that in your industry some of the top people can't pronounce simple words properly. Tom Brokaw can't say his R's correctly. Barbara Walters has trouble with her L's, and Chris Wallace can't say W's. Let me talk to whomever is in charge."
The call is transferred to the CEO who answers, "Hawoe..."

Teacher: Name something that Louis the Fourteenth was responsible for.
Student: Louis the Fifteenth.

At the audition an actor says, "Don't worry. I can handle this part. I've had similar parts in several off-Broadway productions."

The director says, "Off-Broadway...that's great. Where?"
The actor says, "Dubuque."

The little Dutch boy has just saved the town by plugging a hole in the dike with his finger. When he goes home, his mother asks him to help with the dishes. He says, "I'm too tired. I had a rough day at the orifice."

I'm not sure what I should do about my taxes this year. The way I've got it figured...if I use the short form, the government gets my money. And if I use the long form, the accountant gets my money.

These are some tough times. I'm not the only one with money problems. My bank returned a sixty-five dollar check marked "INSUFFICIENT FUNDS." I can't believe they don't have sixty-five dollars.

As soon as my kids were old enough to get a job, I suggested that they put a little money into a savings account and one day it would pay off. I was right. Yesterday I borrowed over five hundred dollars from them.

Regarding that chewing gum ad: Why shouldn't they double the pleasure? They've tripled the price.

I guess the reason people prefer golf carts over caddies is because golf carts can't count.

She says: "All my other boyfriends bring candy when they come over."
He says: "Really? I don't see ya passin' any of it around."

TWO WOMEN OVERHEARD AT A CLASS REUNION:
"Did you ever look at a guy and kinda wish you were single again?"
"Yes."
"Who was it?"
"My husband."

"Information? I need the phone number of the Secay Corporation."

"How do you spell that?"

"S as in sea. E as in eye. C as in cue. A as in are. Y as in you."

"Please hold. I'll connect you with my supervisor."

"Doctor, do you have anything that would make me feel younger?"

The doctor says, "If you don't start taking better care of yourself, you'll be lucky just to keep on getting older."

A kid saying his night prayers closes with: "And please, God, will you make Chicago the capitol of Illinois?"

His mother hears this and asks, "Why on earth would you want Chicago to be the capitol of Illinois?"

The kid says, "Because that's what I put down on my test."

In the England of not too many years ago, members of the royal family, and royalty in general, were revered a lot more than they are today. Probably because they were quite straight-faced and a rather formal lot. With that in mind...picture the narrow streets of London in those days. Two chauffeur-driven limos approach each other from opposite directions. Neither can proceed because of the other.

The driver of one limousine sticks his head out the window and yells, "Kindly make way for Her Majesty, Queen Willhemina, Queen of Holland, Empress of the Netherlands and the Dutch East Indies Empire, if you please."

The other chauffeur opens the door of his Rolls Royce and arrogantly walks to the rear of the vehicle. He very ceremoniously opens the rear door to reveal Queen Mary seated there in all her splendor. With much dignity he says, "And this, I suppose, is a pile of manure?"

I always give my wife the royal treatment. When I take her out to eat, it's either to the Burger King or the Dairy Queen.

I guess my brother-in-law has been late for work a few too many times. The company decided not to wait twenty-five years and give him a watch. They're gonna give him an alarm clock now.

He says, "Did you tell the neighbor lady I was a worthless bum?"
She says, "No...I didn't have to. She already knew."

OVERHEARD IN A COFFEE SHOP:
"Did you get the announcer job you applied for at the radio station?"
"N-n-no, they s-said I was t-t-too t-tall."

While he is still in the recovery room, the patient asks the doctor, "Do you know how much the bill for this operation is going to be?"
The doctor says, "You're not strong enough for that right now."

Life is a little slower when you live in a small town. For example, the rush hour traffic reports are reported in the weekly newspaper.

In my opinion, the only time it's better to give than to receive is if the commodity that's being given is advice.

I went to the doctor to get rid of the annoying ringing in my ears. The ringing is gone. Now I've got a dial tone.

He said, "It could be worse. You could have a busy signal."

I don't need major medical. I need a minor miracle.

My neighbor saves money by going to a veterinarian instead of going to a regular doctor. He says it's cheaper, but you feel a little foolish because they make you get on all fours before they will examine you.

While he was there, a couple came in with a new puppy. They named the puppy "Handyman" because it does odd jobs around the house.

A guy with a show horse was telling the vet about his horse's problem. He said, "Sometimes he limps. Sometimes he doesn't. What should I do?"
The vet said, "Next time he doesn't limp, sell him."

Because so many of the polls taken recently were not very accurate, pollsters have begun making less risky predictions. One poll predicted: "If the elections were held today, they would be seven months early."

I decided to get scientific about my fishing, so I kept a record of all my outings. It turns out that there are two times when the fishing is really good. Before I get there and after I leave.

Forget about bringing home fish...all that time I'm out on the water and I don't even come home with a tan. Last summer the only thing I had that was tan was my front lawn.

My neighbor told me that he can't go fishing with me because he has to stay home and prune his trees. What a waste of time. I looked those trees over pretty good, and I didn't see a single prune.

What I need is some excitement in my life. Anymore, I have more fun remembering what I used to do, than doing what I do do now.

Maybe I'm just out of shape. Lately I get winded getting out of bed.

It was clear that I needed to get some exercise, so I decided to buy that Richard Simmons video: "Sweatin' To The Oldies." So far the only change I've noticed is my voice got higher.

Talk about stress. I'll tell you how much stress there is in my life. You know those coin changers that hang on your belt? I got one that dispenses Rolaids.

Somehow things never go as I want them to go. Even as a kid the only game I was ever any good at was "Follow The Loser."

I used to play cops and robbers, with real cops.

I was very lucky, however, in at least one area. When I was in school, I never got hooked on smoking. Mostly because, every time I tried to sneak a smoke in the bathroom, someone would sneak up and tip it over.

A CORPORATION'S PERSONNEL OFFICER INTERVIEWS A JOB APPLICANT:
He asks, "Where did you get your education?"
The guy says, "Yale."
He asks, "What's your name?"
The guy says, "Yim Yohnson."

An employee is being questioned about some money that was taken from the cash register. The boss says, "How can you claim you're not guilty when there are five people who say that they saw you take the money?"
The guy says, "Oh yea? Well, I can show you five hundred people who will say they didn't see me take it."

CRIMINAL: An opportunistic person with aggressive predatory instincts who doesn't have enough money to start a corporation.

My neighbor stays awake nights thinking of ways to become successful. Personally, I think he'd have more luck if he stayed awake days.

There is a real close correlation between getting up in the morning and getting up in the world.

He said he was going to invest in one of those get-rich-quick schemes. He says it's just getting started so he can "get in" on a shoestring and he can easily triple his investment. Personally, I wonder why anyone would want that many shoestrings.

Actually he isn't lazy...he's religious. He tries to live his life like they do in that parable where the multitude loafs and fishes.

Speaking of that: One of the guys who attended the Sermon on the Mount comes home afterwards and asks his wife, "What's for supper?"

She says, "Loaves and fishes."
He says, "Just my luck. That's what I had for lunch."

Someone asked Anita Loos how she could write: GENTLEMEN PREFER BLONDS when she's a brunette. She said, "That's how I know."

CORRECTION: In last week's paper we erroneously reported on a new record breaking javelin throw of 190 feet. We have since learned that the throw didn't count, because the guy actually threw the javelin only 150 feet, and the guy that the javelin hit, crawled the other 40 feet.

My wife loves sports. In fact, she was once hired by the coach of a professional hockey team to teach the players how to fight dirty.

We fight constantly. The other day I said, "It's three days since we've had an argument."
She says, "It's been four."
I say, "Three"; she says, "Four." Pretty soon we're back at it again.

Her whole family hates me. During the wedding ceremony when they ask, "Is there anyone here who objects to this marriage?" Her side of the family stood up and started forming a double line.

Yesterday somebody asked me what I did before I was married. I said, "Anything I wanted to."

Now I find out that our marriage counselor is getting a divorce.

This marriage counselor is a wimp. He tries to be all things to all people. She tells her side of the story and he says, "She's right."
Then I tell my side of the story and the guy says, "You're right too."
Then my wife says, "We can't both be right."
He says, "How right you are."

I don't mind her having the last word, but she never gets to it.

My pet name for her is "Hon." That's short for: "Attila the Hon."

Speaking of pets...My neighbor was telling me that his dog can say its own name. I asked him what his dog's name is. He said, "Aarf."

The other day I saw this guy trying to buy medicine in the drug store. He told the pharmacist, "I need some of that medicine. I can't think of the name right now, but it sounds like that city in England."

The pharmacist said, "London? Southhampton? Coventry? Liverpool?..."

The guy says, "That's it. Carter's Little Liverpools."

When I was in grade school, the teacher was adamant about the correct use of the words "can" and "may." One time I raised my hand and asked, "Can I go to the bathroom?" She said, "Did you say 'can?'" I told her, "No, I said 'bathroom.'"

My brother-in-law was telling me that he has several great qualities, but the quality that he likes most about himself is the fact that he is always very understanding when he makes a mistake.

Once he opened a restaurant that specialized in submarine sandwiches. You could say that, in a sense, he was successful. It went under.

He made two big mistakes. His first mistake was opening the business. His second mistake was opening it in a fireproof building.

When most people order checks from the bank, the bank automatically prints their name and address on the checks. In my brother-in-law's case they also automatically print: "Insufficient Funds."

"Two guys are talking in a local pub, solving all the world's problems. One of them poses the question: "If you were alone in your car and being chased by some guys from a motorcycle gang, at seventy miles an hour, what would you do?"

The other guy says, "Eighty."

When my daughter talks on the telephone she talks for over an hour. Yesterday she hung up after only thirty minutes. I asked her how come. She said, "Wrong number."

I might be able to get a discount when I order my new license plates now that my uncle is one of the guys who makes them.

First the judge looked at my uncle and said, "Guilty or not guilty?"
Then my uncle looked at his attorney and said, "If he doesn't know, why should we tell him?"

This is the same uncle who once invented a device that cuts four loaves of bread at one time. He called it the four-loaf cleaver.

It was eighty-seven degrees out when I passed a friend on the street. the other day. I said, "You're looking rather cool today."
He said, "You don't look so hot yourself."

I've been thinking about it and I now feel that the company that makes my socks should switch designers with the company that makes my shorts, because my socks sag and my shorts creep up.

HELPFUL HINT FOR THE HOMEMAKER:
You can remove ink stains from a silk dress with an ordinary scissors.

I often think of the various pieces of advice my dad would give to me. He would say things like: "Never give candy to a stranger."

TYPICAL FATHER/SON DIALOGUE...IF DAD IS ALSO READING THE PAPER:
"Dad, can I go outside and watch the solar eclipse."
"Okay, but don't get too close."

When the FBI asked Willie Sutton why he decided to rob banks, he said, "Because that's where they keep the money."

And then there was the warden who was also a bit of a practical joker. He put a thumbtack on the electric chair.

OVERHEARD ON THE GOLF COURSE: "Yes, it's true. Wally took Bob's advice and now he's almost a millionaire. The part you don't understand is that before he took Bob's advice he WAS a millionaire."

This scene takes place in New York City. A guy is telling his wife: "I'm going down to the corner store to pick up some munchies. Cover me."

Speaking of munchies...All this time I thought Limburger cheese was exported from Germany. It's not. It's deported.

I'm not sure how many tons of Limburger they send over here each year, but it's quite a phew.

HUSBAND TO WIFE AS HE TURNS ON THE FIRST FOOT-BALL GAME OF THE YEAR: "Is there anything you want to say before the season starts?"

I was reading about a farmer who doubled his egg production with a sign on the hen house that read: "An egg a day keeps Colonel Sanders away."

Did you ever notice that the husbands of the ten best-dressed women are never on the list of the ten best-dressed men?

I've got a shirt for every day of the week. It's blue.

A lot of antique dealers charge you extra if they have to stand there and listen to you tell them about what your mother used to have.

I had intended to devote the entire column this week to listing reasons why it's important to stick with your decisions, but I changed my mind.

OUR THOUGHT FOR THE DAY: If the meek actually do inherit the earth, how long do you figure they're going to stay meek?

I went to the doctor with a bad case of food poisoning. He charged me thirty dollars to tell me, "It's probably just something you ate."

I was reading in some magazine that the average person goes to the doctor about once a year, and the average doctor goes to the Bahamas about twice a year.

When I was in high school, my parents dreamed that some day I would become a doctor. Later it became rather obvious to them that I could never be a doctor...'cause I couldn't even make the school golf team.

The *Washington Post* has learned of a memo that Abraham Lincoln wrote which leads them to believe that Lincoln may be the cause of all the unproductiveness in our government. He wrote it just prior to going to the Ford Theater. The memo says, "Don't do anything until I get back."

SAFETY TIP: Wait one hour before going into the water after eating. [Three days if you had sponge cake.]

Am I missing something or what? I just noticed that there's a setting on our iron for "Permanent Press."

Down in Australia the word is that boomerangs are making a comeback.

Last week my neighbor came home in a new Cadillac. The very next day the dealer came and took it back. He had the thing for one lousy day. Well...he always said, "One day I'm gonna own a Cadillac."

I always felt that he had little chance of making anything of himself but I was wrong. He has NO chance of making anything of himself.

He's only been at his new job a week and already he's a month behind.

Some pre-teen-aged kids had stopped at the Dodgeville post office and were curious about the "Wanted" posters hanging on the post office wall. One kid asked, "Can't they find any of these guys?"

The clerk said, "They are all on the loose and are wanted by the FBI."

The kid paused for a few seconds and then asked, "Why didn't they just hang on to them when they took their pictures?" [True]

A few weeks ago I was watching *America's Most Wanted* on television. They did an interview with one of the guys that they helped catch. Asked why he robbed banks, he said, "I just wanted to be wanted."

In my opinion the nightly news on television is a big waste of time. It's the same news every night. It just happens to different people.

OUR NEW SLOGAN IS: "All The News That Fits, We Print."

It has been predicted that California will have well over twenty-five million cars on their roads next year. People in that state are advised: "If you want to cross the street, you'd better do it now."

At the hotels in Newark, NJ a room with a view is ten dollars less.

And here in Wisconsin they are doing their best to make the dog tracks successful. They even have restaurants at the track. At the one where I ate, the food wasn't all that great. I was never quite sure if I was eating the entree or an entry.

One time we were eating out at a Chinese restaurant. After the meal the waiter brought a plate of fortune cookies to the table. Mine said, "In the very near future you will pay an outrageous amount for a meal."

The other day my neighbor was out in his yard with a very puzzled look on his face. It turns out he had just bought a hammock and was trying to set it up, when he realized that he only has one tree.

A weary mother finally got her kids quieted down and tucked into bed. With a sigh of relief she went into the bathroom and started to shampoo her hair. And then, just as she got the suds worked up in a good lather, all hell broke loose in the kids' bedroom. That did it! She had had it! She ran into the bedroom ranting and raving, and at the top of her lungs restored peace and quiet. Then she stormed out of the room. For a while there was silence. Then one of the kids whispered, "Who was that?"

I was in a line of people getting onto an airplane. As each person was about to enter the doorway, the flight attendant said, "Watch your head." When she got to me, she said, "Watch your stomach."

OVERHEARD IN COURT:
"Did you or didn't you take the fruit from the fruit stand?"
"Well, actually I did take it, your honor. But I took it by mistake."
"What do you mean by that?"
"I thought it was fresh."

If golf had never been invented, how would they measure hail?

If basketball had never been invented, where would they hold all the high school dances?

Our high school basketball team wasn't very good. At most of the games even the cheerleaders left early.

The team's motto was: "We'll get 'em next time!"

Senior year I was voted president of the stupid council.

Speaking of stupid...I found out that my brother-in-law got a letter from General Motors. GM had issued a recall on his car because of

94

some missing parts. He wrote back and told them that the bank beat them to it...because of some missing payments.

AUTO MECHANIC TO OWNER:
"Let me put it this way. If your car was a horse, we'd have to shoot it."

My advice is to keep the oil and change the car.

A clothing store that had been in business fifty years was holding a big Fifty Year Anniversary Sale. Their ads mentioned drastic price cuts. On the day of the big sale, people showed up long before the doors were scheduled to be opened. As opening time neared, the line was quite long and the people were rather protective about holding their place in line. One old guy kept pushing his way up to the front of the line. Each time the people pushed him back to the end of the line. Finally the guy says, "If they do that one more time, I'm not gonna open the store."

When my brother-in-law was going to high school, he spent two years at Hoover High School and two years at West High School. As a result, both schools make claims as to where he got his education. Hoover claims he got it at West, and West claims he got it at Hoover.

At our annual family picnic I asked him what he'd like on his hot dog. He said, "A hamburger."

In response to comments that I injured my typing finger, my wife said, "I read the stuff that you've been typing. You don't have a typewriter. You've got a tripewriter."

If the truth be known, I actually wish that my wife was a feminist. Then she'd hate all men, not just me.

The local policeman is no Sherlock Holmes. There was a robbery in town and he reported to the chief that he..."already has one of the guys."

The chief asked, "Which one?"
He said, "The one that was robbed."

OUR THOUGHT FOR THE DAY:
Though he's not very humble, there's no police like Holmes.

The phone rings and, in a whisper, a six-year-old boy says, "Hello."
The caller says, "Can I talk to your mother?"
The kid whispers, "She's outside."
The caller says, "Can I talk to your father?"
The kid whispers, "He's outside too."
The caller says, "Is there anyone else there?"
The kid whispers, "The police are here."
The caller says, "The police are at your house?"
The kid whispers, "Yea. They're outside."
The caller says, "What's everybody doing outside?"
The kid whispers, "Looking for me."

I could never understand how all the car dealers could make any money selling their cars at "Invoice" sales. Well, I finally figured it out. They don't make money selling the cars. They make money fixing them.

When I was just a kid, I used to wonder where the sun went each night. Night after night, I'd lay in bed thinking about it. Then one night I stayed awake all night long trying to figure it out. And in the morning it dawned on me.

I get up early every morning. Just like clock-work, at five fifteen I'm out of bed, go to the bathroom, back in bed...five seventeen.

When my wife goes to Las Vegas, her philosophy is: "The less you bet, the more you lose if you win."

Q. Why did the chicken cross the road?
A. To show the raccoon that it could be done.

More and more people, lately, make sure that every Sunday they take time to bow their heads. Not to pray. To putt.

REGARDING LENDING MONEY TO A FRIEND:
An optimist is someone who will.
A pessimist is someone who won't.
A cynic is someone who did.

The guy golfing behind me said that he had been watching me all day, and he thinks I'm standing too close to the ball. I told him that he might be right because I've always had a poor stance when I tee off. He said, "No, I mean you're too close to the ball AFTER you tee off."

I'm really worried. I just bought a great big life insurance policy and today my horoscope says, "A recent investment is about to pay off."

There are many things these days, that aren't what they used to be. They bothered me so much that I decided to make a list. My wife said, "Don't forget to include yourself."

A guy asks the druggist, "Do you do these urinalysis tests here?"
The druggist says, "Yes."
The guy says, "Well, wash your hands and give me a bottle of vitamins."

A grade school political science teacher asks if anyone knows how long members of the United States Congress can serve. A kid in the back says, "Until they get caught."

My brother-in-law was telling me that when he was a kid they used to live next to a mean lady. She used to say things like: "You little brat. What are you doing walking in on me while I'm in the tub?"

What a guy! One time he tried to mail a pot roast with food stamps.

Psychiatrists tell us that most women tend to marry men who are like their fathers. My brother-in-law's wife adds: "That's why the mothers always cry at weddings."

A court case involves voting fraud. The judge says to the defendant, "You're charged with voting seven times. Do you have anything to say?"

The guy says, "Charged? I thought I was getting paid!"

REMEMBER: The sum total of the national debt is really some total.

Let me see if I got this straight. They spend $60,000 on a school bus so the kids don't have to walk to school, and then they spend $800,000 on a gymnasium so the kids can get some exercise?

A kid visiting his grandparents in Texas gets to meet a real cowboy who is sitting on a real horse. The following conversation takes place:
"Why do you guys wear those big hats?"
"To keep the sun out of our eyes when we're out on the trail."
"Why do you guys wear those handkerchiefs around your neck?"
"When it's dusty, we pull 'em up over our nose to keep the dust out."
"Why do you wear that leather stuff over your pants?"
"The chaps protect our legs from the thorns when we're in the brush."
"How come you wear tennis shoes?"
"So people can tell us apart from truck drivers."

Back in the old days most of the cowboys were the strong silent type. They didn't ask questions. They'd shoot first and ask questions later. Of course, using that system, they also didn't get too many answers.

In fact, the following was heard outside the fort one night as one of these strong, silent cowboy types was on sentry duty:
"BANG! BANG, BANG!"
"Who went there?"

Today this would never happen. These days we have a system of laws. Even a murderer is assumed to be innocent until proven insane.

An old gent puts two quarters into the automatic coffee machine at the bus depot. He pushes the button marked: "Coffee with cream and sugar." The machine starts humming. Normally a cup drops down into the opening, but the cup sticks. He watches as the coffee comes out of the tube and goes right into the drain. He watches as the cream comes out of the tube and goes right into the drain. He watches the sugar come out of the tube and go straight into the drain. Finally the action stops and the old guy stands there for a minute, looking. Then he says, "How do you like that? It even drinks it for you."

THOUGHT FOR THE DAY:
Kleptomaniacs help themselves because they can't help themselves.

Did you ever notice that to a teenage girl it's not really "true love" if her parents approve.

MARRIAGE COUNSELOR TO A COUPLE IN FOR COUNSELING:
"Marriage is a lot like bath water. After you're in it for awhile, it's not so hot."

The twenty-fifth wedding anniversary is a real tough one to deal with. It's too soon to brag and too late to complain.

My neighbor was telling me that for five years after they got married his mother-in-law lived with them. He said that it wasn't easy to take, but he couldn't do anything about it because it was her house.

In all those years he said that he and his mother-in-law never had any disputes. I notice that he still cowers at the mere mention of her name. He says, "The woman was big enough to fight grizzly bears with a stick."

What times we live in. Fast food restaurants, overnight express mail, FAX machines. We have become a very efficient society. In fact, even at the beach you only have to look half as long to see twice as much.

We've been able to improve on just about everything except people.

I have met various people over the years who were very enthusiastic about hard work. Just my luck...they were all people I worked for.

I admit that I'm confused by all the presidential campaigning. I can't tell who's actually working up a steam and who's just generating a fog.

THOUGHT FOR THE DAY:
To eliminate the misery of a hangover, drink coffee the night before instead of the morning after.

A young sailor taking naval survival training refuses to jump from a fifteen foot high platform into the water below. The instructor takes him aside and says, "Son, what would you do if you were on the deck of a sinking ship, fifteen feet above the water and ordered to abandon ship?"
The sailor says, "I'd wait until it sank ten more feet."

You can profit from your mistakes. Have a garage sale.

Dazed but delighted, the father of triplets walks into the hospital nursery trying to find them among all the newborn babies in the room.
The nurse hollers, "You can't come in here; you're not sterile."
The proud papa says, "You can say that again!"

OVERHEARD IN THE SUPERMARKET CHECK-OUT LINE:
"It appears as though my daughter doesn't want to get married."
"That's what you think. Just wait until the wrong boy comes along."

The angry father says, "Can you give me one good reason why you are coming home at five o'clock in the morning?"
The son says, "Breakfast?"

At a twenty-year class reunion, two guys are talking about the recent arrest of one of the classmates. The conversation goes like this:
"The way I understand it, Lenny was arrested for merely saying things behind people's backs. I wonder what on earth it was that he said?"
"I think it was, 'Stick 'em up.'"

You know that you're getting old when it's the doctor, not the police, warning you to slow down.

Want to have a little fun with your doctor? The next time the doctor asks you to get undressed...say, "You first."

THOUGHT FOR THE DAY:
Knowledge is power...if you know it about the right person.

Watching those track and field events during the Olympics, I could not help but think about what rotten shape my high school track team was in. In fact, that entire conference was in terrible shape. I'm pretty sure it was the only conference, ever, where the hundred-yard dash was a relay.

The rules at the country club state that a person cannot golf unless he becomes a member. So my neighbor became a member. The rule is wrong. I've seen him on the green a few times since then. He still can't golf.

When I first moved into this area, I had only two dollars to my name. Today I owe thousands.

I read in last week's paper about Gary Grinnell's luck in the lottery so I decided to call and ask if he'd lend me forty-five hundred dollars. He said that he only won forty-four hundred dollars. I told him that he could owe me the rest.

During half-time at the football game, I was in the concession line behind some guy who just bought two beers, a Diet pepsi, two Seven-Ups, four bags of popcorn and a Snickers bar. He was having trouble trying to carry it all back to his seat. They even offered to give the guy a tray, but he said, "No thanks, I've got too much to carry as it is."

PSYCHIATRIST TO PATIENT: This idea of yours, that everybody hates you, is absolutely ridiculous. Not everybody has met you.

SOUTHERN DOCTOR TO PATIENT:
"Open your mouth and say, 'Ahhh.. will not sue.'"

It's all getting so complicated. These days you can't simply bribe a politician. You have to submit a sealed bid.

TODAY'S WORDS WORTH REMEMBERING:
A loaded gun is a very dangerous thing, but it's even more dangerous if the person carrying it is also loaded.

A woman is after a talent agent to listen to her twelve-year-old son play the piano. She says, "He sounds just like Paderewski."

The agent says, "I'm sorry. I don't have time."

The woman says, "I have a tape you can listen to. It will just take a few minutes. My son is only twelve and he sounds just like Paderewski."

The agent realizes that the best way to get rid of her is to listen to the tape. To his surprise, it is beautiful. It brings tears to his eyes. The agent says, "That is wonderful. I can't believe that it's your son."

The woman says, "No, on the tape, that's Paderewski. But my son sounds just like him."

An extravagance is anything you buy that your spouse has no use for.

One time I won a trip to China. It was okay, I guess, but it took me close to eighteen months to win a trip back home.

In my mail box last week was a letter to The Village Idiot with no other address. The phrase "village idiot" didn't bother me all that much. What bothered me was the fact they knew where to deliver it.

And then there was the guy who, after his wife gave birth to a third set of twins, divorced her on the grounds that she was over bearing.

A woman confesses to her husband, "When your job kept you away for several nights at a time, I couldn't stand to be alone. So now I have to tell you that, once in a while, I was unfaithful."

The husband is shocked. He asks her, "Was it with my friend Ernie?"

The wife says, "No, it wasn't with Ernie."

He asks, "Was it with my friend Al?"

She says, "No, it wasn't with Al either."

The husband says, "Not with my friend Lou, I hope?"
The wife says, "Hey, I've got some friends of my own ya know."

WATCH: A device worn on the wrist, used to determine how late you are.

My doctor is very dedicated to his profession. One time he was called on an emergency. He literally ran through the last three holes.

In the post office, an elderly woman approached the clerk and asked him if he would please address an envelope for her. The clerk said that he'd be happy to. When he had finished, she asked if he would write out a short note to enclose in the envelope. The clerk wrote the short note.
The clerk then asked, "Is there anything else I can do for you?"
The woman looked the note over and said, "At the bottom would you add, 'P.S. Please excuse the handwriting'?"

A few years ago I signed up for this retirement plan. They said that if I make all the payments, I can retire on twenty-four hundred a month. It sounded real good, and then today I finally read all the small print. It's not twenty-four hundred dollars. It's twenty-four hundred calories.

CONVICT COMPLAINING TO THE GUARD:
"Maybe you're not aware of it, but the judge sent me to this prison for the rest of my life. Every day you guys get me out of bed early, and you've got me out there breaking rocks with a sledge hammer. Some rest!"

A guy applies for a job with a clothing store. He tells the manager, "I really need this job. Please give me a chance. I can sell anything."
The manager says, "Let's see how good you are." He shows the guy a suit that has been in stock for years. IT IS UGLY! Nobody could sell it. He tells the salesman, "If you sell this suit, you've got the job."
The guy goes to work, and the manager goes out for lunch. When the manager returns, the new salesman, with his clothes all torn and bloody, tells him, "I sold the suit."

The manager is absolutely elated, but noticing the condition the guy's clothes are in, the manager asks, "Did you have a lot of resistance from the customer?"

The guy says, "No, I didn't have any trouble from the customer, but I got some major resistance from his seeing eye dog."

Here's something that has been bothering me lately. I have to wonder if bankers can really count. Every time I go into the bank I notice that they have six windows and two tellers.

All kidding aside. I feel a warm, personal sentiment towards my bank. Why not? The bank pays more interest to me than my wife does.

REMEMBER:
Gambling away the rent money can be a moving experience.

It's now September and the schools are open. So look out for the kids. Especially if they're driving.

These kids squeal the tires each time they pull away from a stop sign. They must think rubber grows on trees.

In English class one kid is trying to figure out if the word "slacks" is singular or plural. The kid next to him says, "As far as I can tell, they're singular on the top and plural at the bottom."

For years I was my own worst critic, then I got married.

In a crack-down on gambling, six guys are arrested for shooting craps. In court the judge says, "I want all you crap-shooters to come up here." The six guys walk to the front of the court, and they're joined by a guy from the back of the room. The judge asks the extra guy why he came up. The guy says, "I can shoot craps."

The other day my neighbor was wearing one beige, over-the-calf sock and one brown, ankle-high sock. I pointed this out to him, and kind of expected him to use that old line: "I have another pair of socks at home just like these." He didn't. What he said was: "These are a matched set, but one of them faded and the other one shrunk."

What a guy. He thinks the capital of Minnesota is "M."

A beautiful young woman asks the grocer how much six apples will cost. The grocer is a bit of a wolf. He says, "Each one will cost one kiss."

The woman says, "Okay, wrap 'em up. My grandmother will pay you."

CORRECTION: Last week, in comments about members of the U.S. Congress, the words "are committed" were used to describe them. That was an error. It was supposed to have read, "should be committed."

There is one good thing about my brother-in-law. He is honest. For one entire summer he worked in a bath house and never took a bath.

I'm an optimist. I can see good in everything. Well, almost everything. I don't see good in the dark.

Talk about not seeing in the dark. One time I crashed my car into the back of a police car and woke up two cops.

A five-year-old is riding in the car with his father. As they approach each turn, the father turns the turn signal on. Before long the kid says, "What's that clicking noise I keep hearing?"

The father says, "That's the turn signal. I turn it on so people will know when I'm going to turn."

The little guy thinks about this for a few seconds and then suggests, "There's no way they're gonna hear it."

Question: What's the penalty for bigamy?
Answer: Two mothers-in-law.

Yes, it's true. Husbands tell a lot of lies, but it's the wife's fault. They ask the questions.

My wife says that there are two kinds of secrets. Those that are not worth keeping and those that are too good to keep.

Every so often I come up with a great idea. Example: I got my wife a very expensive set of china. Now she doesn't trust me to do the dishes.

A man walking down the street passes a house. On the porch he notices a little kid who is too short to reach the doorbell. No matter how much the little guy stretches, he just can't reach it. The man tells the kid, "Let me get that for you." He goes up onto the porch and rings the bell.

The kid looks up at the man and says, "Okay, now let's run."

Last week on a television talk show, some guy quoted Will Rogers's famous line: "I never met a man I didn't like."

Under her breath my wife mumbled, "He obviously never dated any."

The neighbor couple had another great big argument. I'm certain I know what their problem is. It's the same old "failure to communicate" thing. He won't tell her who he's dating.

Some guys abuse their wives...by staying married to them.

Question: What do you get if you play a country song backwards?

Answer: You get your girlfriend back, your dog back, your job back...

Talking to the congregation about helping the poor, the minister said, "You were put on this earth to help others."

A little kid in the back of the church poked his mother and whispered, "What were the others put here for?"

I know how it feels to be poor. When we were kids, our family was poor. To make ends meet my mother used to take in washing from the neighbors...and keep it.

One thing my mother always insisted is that I put on a clean pair of socks every day. I guess I didn't understand. After about the fifth day, I couldn't even get my shoes on.

One time my parents went to some discount store where television sets were on sale. The salesman told my dad, "You make a small down payment and then you don't make any more payments for six months."

My dad said, "Who told you about us?"

Then there's the fast food chain that offers prunes on the menu at the drive up window. They figure it's the perfect food to go.

After the opening night performance of a new Broadway play the star of the show goes to her dressing room and complains to her manager when she finds that only fourteen flower bouquets were sent to her dressing room. Her manager tries to pacify her saying, "That's wonderful. You should be honored that fourteen bouquets were sent to you."

The prima donna says, "Why should I be honored? I paid for fifteen."

A woman is doing her laundry in a laundromat when a guy comes in and starts to do his laundry in the very next machine. They start to talk. Soon he asks her for a date. She says, "I don't date perfect strangers."

He says, "No problem. I'm not perfect."

THROUGH THE FENCE A DOG IS TALKING TO THE DOG NEXT DOOR:

"I finally got the guy I live with trained so that whenever I sit up he gives me a treat."

The most important thing about training a dog is that you have to know more than the dog.

Talk about smart dogs. A local farmer was telling me that he has a dog, twenty-seven cows and a large wooded pasture. He says that, twice a day, this dog goes out to the large wooded pasture and finds every one of the twenty-seven cows, and brings them in for milking. Last week he sold one of the cows. The next day at milking time, that dog went out and brought in twenty-six cows and went back out to look for the twenty-seventh cow. He says the dog went from the barn to the pasture and back so many times that he finally had to stop what he was doing and show the dog the check that he got for the cow, before the dog would stop looking for it.

The other day my neighbor went to the doctor for some kind of checkup. One of the questions the doctor asked him was, "Do you drink coffee?"

My neighbor said, "Yes."

The doctor asked, "How much?"

My neighbor said, "About twenty-four or twenty-five cups a day."

The doctor said, "Doesn't that keep you awake?"

My neighbor said, "It helps."

This is one guy who is not too eager to get out of bed in the morning. At his house...even his smoke alarm has a "snooze button."

The guy who was snapping the photographs at their company picnic asked my windy brother-in-law if he wanted a large picture or a small picture.

My brother-in-law said, "Just a small picture."

The guy said, "Then close your mouth."

He has relatives living in Lithuania who are very happy that they are no longer a part of Russia. He says they hated those Russian winters.

TEN STAGES OF AMBITION:
1. To say mama.
2. To crawl to mama.
3. To walk by yourself.
4. To be just like your dad.
5. To become an airline pilot.
6. To become a famous rock star.
7. To become a multi-millionaire.
8. To marry the woman of your dreams.
9. To try to make it on what little you earn.
10. To hang on long enough so you can draw a pension.

My wife belongs to this club called: "The Vicious Circle."

One of their members was once arrested for attacking a pit bull.

———

When they reach the assigned cruising altitude, the pilot of a certain airline comes out of the cabin and strolls down the aisle to welcome the passengers. He passes a little old lady who's on her very first airplane flight. He greets her with, "Nice to have you on board. I am your pilot. Where are you headed?" The woman turns white and says, "I thought you knew!"

———

VETERAN NURSE TO NEW NURSE:
"Would you be very upset if we called you by some kind of a nickname? The doctors get nervous when they hear the word, 'Sue.'"

———

OVERHEARD: He not only lied to me about his yacht, but he made me row.

———

An old retired ship's captain is telling his young grandson about some of his adventures on the sea. He says, "The fog had been quite thick all night, but all at once I could make out a hazy glow. Soon it got closer. Finally I was able to make out what it was I was looking at. It was the end of my cigar."

———

The teacher asks a third grader, "If you had a big piece of candy and a small piece of candy, and had to share one of them with your brother, which piece would you give him?"
The kid asks, "Do you mean my big brother or my little brother?"

———

I may have made a big error in judgment awhile back. This guy I used to work with wanted to borrow a couple hundred dollars. He said he would then have enough money for the plastic surgery he's been wanting to get. So like a big dummy I lent him the money, and he has never paid me back. What's worse is I haven't seen him around lately and now I realize that, even if I do, I don't have any idea what he looks like.

———

I asked my neighbor if he tints his hair. He said, "No, it was that color when I bought it."

———

His toupee looks like it made a forced landing on his head.

ADVICE FOR MARRIED COUPLES:
If your mate turns fifty and asks, "Do you think I really look fifty?"
Don't say, "No, but you used to."

A Wisconsin girl and a girl from Georgia end up as college
roommates. One day they got to talking about guys.
The Wisconsin girl says, "As far as I'm concerned, guys are all
alike."
The Georgia girl says, "They're all ah like too."

HUSBAND TO WIFE AS THEY ENTER MATERNITY WARD:
"Honey, are you sure you want to go through with this?"

The well-to-do and socially prominent father is having a talk with
his daughter's boyfriend. He says, "Son, anyone who marries my
daughter will need a lot of money."
The boyfriend says, "Then I'd be perfect sir. I do."

My neighbor's kid wants to play guitar in a rock band. He went out
and spent some really big bucks on amplifiers and stuff. I wondered
where he could get that kind of money. Then one day I heard him play.
Now I know. He probably used the money his parents gave him for
music lessons.

TITLE TO A ROCK SONG:
"How Can I Miss You If You Won't Go Away?"

The youngster handed his report card to his father, as well as, one of
his father's old report cards that he'd found in a box up in the attic.
The little guy felt rather secure until his father said, "This report
card of mine isn't any better than yours. I guess the only fair thing to
do is give you what my father gave me."

ONE PROUD POLITICIAN TO ANOTHER:
"My kid broke his first promise today."

DOCTOR'S ANSWERING MACHINE MESSAGE:

"The doctor is on vacation now. You need to eat more sensibly and get proper exercise and sufficient rest. After the tone leave your name and your billing address. Please call for another appointment in a month."

This guy I used to know could sell anything to anybody. He was smooth. One time he even sold a local farmer two milking machines and the farmer only had one cow. And then he took the cow in on trade.

I am against converting to the metric system. It would totally mess up some of our most colorful phrases. An example of what I'm talking about: One old adage converts to: "A miss is as good as 1.61 kilometers."

The new fad in business lunches is: "You are served in ten minutes or your next lunch is free." I was just at one restaurant that didn't offer such a guarantee. At this place, you're lucky to get: "Same day service."

I waited for what seemed like forever. When the waiter finally did bring my food, I asked him if he was the same waiter who took my order.

He said, "Yes."

I said, "I thought you'd be a lot older by now."

Local law enforcement officials claim they're trying to stop gambling. They feel that it will not be a very easy thing to do, however, because it's really got them hooked.

There is one civic minded community I heard about that regularly holds huge raffles, and the proceeds go to the city's anti-gambling campaign.

The president of their local school board, who is against the raffles, bet the mayor fifty bucks that the whole thing was a big waste of time.

During the early years of my life I didn't gamble at all. I progressed very slowly when I was young because of poor role models. For example, when I was in sixth grade, my dad told me that he'd buy me a sling shot if I'd stop sucking my thumb.

I wasn't like the other ten-year-old, sixth grade kids. I was twelve.

I was a rather disruptive kid in school, and got into lots of trouble. There was one area, however, where I made my parents very happy, but not the teachers. In fact, my teachers resented my perfect attendance record.

I came from a rather large family, and my parents seemed to have at least one hyperactive, obnoxious kid in every grade. Eventually it got so bad that the teachers took up a collection to buy my dad a vasectomy.

The ardent golfer places his ball on the tee and turns to grab a club, finding himself face-to-face with a woman wearing a long wedding dress. He sheepishly says, "I told you, 'only if it rains.'"

The doctor is examining a new patient, and notices numerous scratches and bruises on the man's shins. He asks, "Are you some kind of football or hockey player?"
The guy says, "No. My wife doesn't like the way I play bridge."

OVERHEARD DURING MARRIAGE COUNSELING:
"Well, if I'm big enough to admit your faults, you should be too."

My wife and I stopped at a quaint little motel in northern Wisconsin. The desk clerk asked us if we wanted a room with a tub or a shower.
I asked, "What's the difference?"
He said, "With a tub you sit. With a shower you stand."

Here's a beauty. The other night my neighbor called the pizza place to have a large pizza delivered to his house. He gave them his address and the name of the street he lives on. They asked, "How do you spell that?" He said, "My wife helps me."

Is he something or what? You could use him for a blueprint if you were building an idiot.

One time he tried to explain to me that baseball teams could eliminate all those controversial close plays if they would just move first base a foot or so further away.

The airline's regulation that bans passengers from smoking on flights doesn't go far enough. I think it should also apply to the engines.

FLASHLIGHT: A place to store dead batteries.

In the year 1626, Peter Minuit bought the island of Manhattan for $24. Today it costs more than that just to park there.

OVERHEARD DURING A BUSINESS LUNCH:
"A guy I know made a few investments with some money he had inherited from a miserly old uncle. He now has a small fortune."
"Oh, that's good."
"No, that's not so good. He inherited a large fortune."

There is an old saying: "Misers may not be very much fun to live with, but they make extremely good ancestors."

STUDENT GETTING RESULTS OF HIS APTITUDE TEST:
"Your test results suggest that your best chance for getting a job is in some field where a close relative has an influential position."

When there is nothing worth watching on television, we open the windows and listen to the neighbors fight. Last week she accused him of being a golf addict. He said, "I am not." She said, "You are too." This went on for twenty minutes. Finally, she got so mad she broke his snow wedge.

He says that she is not very good with names. Well, I totally disagree. You should hear some of the names she calls him.

One time he told me that his car has two air bags. One is compressed inside the steering wheel in front of him, and the other one sits on the seat beside him.

A marriage counselor is becoming very frustrated by the fact that he's getting absolutely no cooperation from a couple who came for counseling. Finally he suggests that each should say one nice thing about the other. Still there's total silence. The counselor says, "We're getting nowhere. There has to be one nice thing that one of you can say about the other." He looks at each of them for a response. The woman thinks a bit longer, then shrugs and says, "His brother is worse."

The treasurer at one of the local service clubs reported that they had only $23.47 left in the treasury. Someone commented, "This is too little for any club of our size." The club treasurer defended the small balance with a comment of his own. "It's about nine billion more than the treasury of the United States has."

Thousands of people in this country aren't working, and that is scary. However, the real problem is that so many of these people are employed.

My neighbor volunteered to stay late at work to run their new machine. He was making big money, but ran into some problems. The machine was the new full color copier. He neglected to tell anybody that he volunteered. And because he somehow activated the automatic enlarger, the big money he was making was about a quarter inch too big.

When he left the company, they gave him a little momentum.

He's always working on some scheme. For the past several months he has been out back in his garage, working on a car that doesn't use gasoline. He said, "It would if I could get it started."

One time he tried to cross a rooster with a rooster, and got a very cross rooster.

What a guy! He told me that he came from a big family. I asked him if he was the oldest. He said, "No. My dad was."

Last year we all went to my brother-in-law's for Thanksgiving dinner. After dinner we retired to the front room and he showed slides of their vacation. They have a huge front room. I'd say it sleeps about sixteen.

I can still remember the first time I watched my mother cook a turkey. It was disgusting. About every half hour she'd open the oven, pull the turkey out, and stick a thermometer into it. I told her, "If you think it's sick, I don't want any."

CORRECTION: In last week's paper we ran a story about a local man who injured himself while fishing. This was an error. We have since learned that it didn't happen while he was fishing. He dislocated his shoulders the next day, while describing a fish that got away.

Talk about having the wrong information. For years I had thought that after my brother-in-law got out of high school, he'd gone to Penn State. Today I found out I had the facts mixed-up. What actually happened was after he got out of high school, he spent several years in the state pen.

A guy buys a very expensive parrot and wants to teach it how to talk. He gives it a prominent place in his home, and every morning he walks up to the cage and says, "Good morning, Polly. How are you feeling today?"
Each morning the bird hears these same words, but never tries to talk. One morning the guy finally gives up on getting the bird to talk, and he walks past the cage without saying anything. The parrot looks up at him and says, "What the heck are you so grumpy about?"

My wife is mad because I came home late and didn't call to tell her where I was. She said, "Where were you? I looked all over town for you."
I said, "Then you should have found me. I was there."

She says the economy will improve now that so many women were elected to public office. Well, she didn't use those exact words. What she said was more like: "Adios, stag-nation."

Shortly after we were married, I asked my wife, "Why can't you learn to make bread like my mother makes?"
She said, "I will, when you learn to make dough like my father makes."

My father was watching one of the TV talk shows and heard them claim, "There are 20% more 75 year-old-women than 75 year-old-men."
He thought about it for awhile and then he mumbled to the television, "At age 75, who cares?"

This last minute item...Bill Bailey called. He's not coming home.

HUSBAND TO WIFE DURING AN ARGUMENT:
"You think I married you because your rich uncle died and left you two million dollars. Admit it. Well, you are wrong. I would have married you no matter who died and left you two million dollars."

My rich uncle didn't leave anything to anybody. He wasn't merely rich. He was filthy rich. Then, just before he died, his investments went sour and he took a bath.

District Attorney: "Do you happen to recall what you were doing between five and six?"
Defendant: "Going to kindergarten."

My wife is one person who can make a long story short. She interrupts.

I've often thought that she'd be good at some kind of job, searching for potential earthquake sites. She's an expert at finding faults.

My neighbor has a horseshoe hanging over his front door. I asked if he figured that it was going to bring him good luck. He said that he didn't believe in all of that superstitious stuff. I said, "Then why hang it over your door, if you don't believe that it will bring you good luck?"

He said, "I read somewhere, that a horseshoe will bring you good luck whether you believe it will or not."

Here's a beauty. Last month he was telling me that he really likes his new boss. He claims to see this new boss more like a buddy than a boss. One night he suggested that the two of them stop for a couple of beers after work. I asked him how it went. He said, "She turned me down."

He was telling me about this really great seafood restaurant he found. The other day I happened to be driving by the place and looked it over. The sign offered a catch-of-the-day special. From the looks of the place I'd say that the catch-of-the-day is hepatitis.

I saw an invitation to one of those "hundred-dollar-a-plate" political fund raising dinners. In very small print, towards the bottom, it reads: "Roquefort dressing 50 cents extra."

My wife's friend was having a problem. Her waist was getting too large. So for several months she bought nothing but those "low-fat" products. It worked. It lowered the fat to her hips.

Life is not simple. You would think that someone could develop a pizza that gives you heartburn immediately, instead of at two in the morning.

I was sitting in my parked car and heard this strange noise behind me, "Ummmm, screech. Ummmm, screech. Ummmm, screech." I turned around to see what was going on. Apparently, some drivers don't understand what to do at a flashing red light.

Two vampire bats wake up in the middle of the night, hungry for blood. The first one says, "Let's fly out of the cave and get some blood."

The second one says, "We're new here. It's dark out, and we don't know where to look. We'd better wait until the other bats go."

The first bat says, "Who needs them? I can find some blood somewhere," and he flies out of the cave. When he returns, he is covered with blood.

The second bat says, "Where did you get the blood?"

The first bat takes the second bat up front to the mouth of the cave. Pointing into the night, he says, "See that black building over there?"

The second bat says, "Yes."

The first bat says, "Well, I didn't."

BOSS TO NEW EMPLOYEE:

"Around here I'm a number, just like everyone else. We're all numbers. The only difference is that I'm number one."

The new employee is called into the boss's office because he is always late for work. The boss says, "Don't you know what time we start to work around here?" The employee says, "No, sir. I've only been here four days, and each time I get here, everybody is already working."

After researching what was often thought to be just an unfounded myth, scientists have now confirmed that fat people are actually good-natured and very easy to get along with. They've also determined that the reason fat people are so good-natured and so easy to get along with is because they can't fight and they can't run.

Here is something I never did understand. The phrase "fat chance" and the phrase "slim chance" mean the same thing.

"Operator, how much is a long distance call to my brother's house?"

"That depends on where your brother lives."

"He lives about a half mile from my house."

"Then it's not a long distance call, and there are no extra charges."

"Well, is there a long distance charge to call my sister?"

"Where does she live?"

"She's living at my house."

"At your house?"

"Yeah. She's with the kids while my wife and I are here in Las Vegas."

A TWISTED TRUISM: One swallow does not a summer make, but it can sure blow a New Year's resolution.

My neighbor finally applied for a job, but I don't think he'll get it. I guess during the interview he was boasting about his super intellect. He said, "I enter a lot of those crossword-puzzle contests, and one time I came real close to winning."
The interviewer said, "That's very nice, but we're looking for someone who can be smart, while they're punched-in, and on the job."
My neighbor said, "I was."

He is something else. Last week his horoscope said: "Be very watchful, because a ton of money is heading your way." He got so excited, when he drove home to tell his wife, he crashed into a Brinks truck.

OUR THOUGHT FOR THE DAY: You know that your team is not very good if the concession stand sells hot dogs "to go."

It's very obvious to me that this is one newspaper that is being read. Last week a local business advertised for a night watchman, and the very next night the place was burglarized.

I think it's time to clean the rug in my office. I got a speckled rug, thinking that the design would kind of hide dirt, so I wouldn't have to vacuum very much. Now I've noticed that some of the speckles are moving, and where the rug meets the molding, it is.

I have trouble at airports. A terrorist can sneak past security with a machine gun, and I get strip-searched if I've taken a vitamin with iron.

Did you ever offer your two cents worth and then wish that you hadn't? One time I was on a flight, sitting next to a couple who got involved in a very intense discussion. I was a little too quick to offer my opinion. It was a bit later I realized that "Roe vs. Wade" has nothing to do with the various methods of crossing a river.

The first thing I do when I get on the airplane is to determine if the person next to me wants to talk. Here's a lesson I learned the hard way. Never wake them up to find out.

On a three hour flight out West I was telling the guy next to me about some problems. I said, "My wife doesn't understand me. How about yours?"

He looked up from the book he was reading and said, "I kinda doubt it. She doesn't even know you."

I'm actually at my best when they serve the food. Timing is everything when you beg. I waited for the right time and then, with as much dignity as the situation would allow I asked, "Are you gonna eat that pickle?"

Another time, after gulping down a Pepsi, I tried a little experiment. It was embarrassing because I really thought that we were traveling faster than the speed of sound, and that somebody seated behind me would get the blame when I burped.

The batter was given the bunt signal. When the next pitch crossed the plate, the batter bunted the ball and raced to first base. When he got there, he heard the umpire yell, "You're out."

The batter yelled back, "I was not out."

The umpire repeated emphatically, "You were out!"

The batter got nose-to-nose with the umpire and said, "I was not out."

The umpire shrugged and said, "Okay, if you don't believe me just take a look at tomorrow's paper."

First it was the movies. Now even TV is showing some rather explicit love scenes. The only thing they leave to the imagination is the plot.

Whenever the kids would misbehave, my wife would use her famous line: "Every time you kids are naughty, I get another gray hair on my head."

Once she used the line when my parents were visiting. The kids looked at their silver-haired grandma and grandpa. Then they looked over at me and one of them said, "Dad must have been a horrible kid."

I told my neighbor, "I got my wife an eight-day clock for Christmas."
He said, "What's an eight-day clock?"
I said, "It runs for eight days without winding."
He said, "How long will it run if you wind it?"

He's always coming up with some unbelievable scheme. This year he said he's going to save some money. He's sending a chain Christmas card.

Every couple of months my wife cleans out the refrigerator, and makes her special "Enthusiastic Stew." She puts everything she has into it.

She is extremely creative when it comes time to use up the leftovers. For dessert we had liver creme pie.

This stuff is terrible. The only thing worse than her liver creme pie, is leftover liver creme pie.

OVERHEARD OUTSIDE CHURCH:
"Did you see the horrible dress Mrs. Olson was wearing?"
"No. I missed it."
"Did you notice Mrs. Miller's dress? It was just about as bad."
"No. I missed that too."
"Naturally, that snooty Mrs. Crandall had to show off her new jacket."
"I didn't see it either. I was dozing off most of the time."
"Dozing off? A lot of good it does you to go to church."

OVERHEARD INSIDE CHURCH:
"Do you take this man to be your lawfully wedded husband?"
"I do."
"Do you take this woman to be your lawfully wedded wife?"
"He does."

My neighbor said he figured his wife was not much of a cook when she kept referring to the oven as: "That square thing in the kitchen."

Attorney: "Yes or no, did you, or did you not, on the date in question, or at anytime, previously or subsequently, state or even intimate to the defendant, or anybody else, either alone or with someone, whether that person was a friend or merely an acquaintance, or, for that matter, even some total stranger, that the statements imputed to you, regardless of whether you deemed them to be just or unjust, and with full knowledge of their being clearly denied by the plaintiff, were considered, by you to be consequential, or merely a matter of no moment? Answer yes or no."
Witness: "Yes or no what?"

"Is this the candy store?"
"Yes, it is."
"Well, I just sent my son, Richie, to your place to purchase two pounds of chocolate covered cherries. When he got back with them, I noticed that the bag felt kinda light. Upon weighing the bag I found that it only had a pound and a half in it."
"Well, I sure don't understand it. My scale is extremely accurate and the clerk is totally honest. Have you tried weighing Richie?"

Some advice for anyone whose son got an electric guitar for Christmas. The music is too loud if it puts ripples in your morning cup of coffee.

WE ARE FIRST TO REPORT THE NEWS:
Last week we had the distinction of being the only area newspaper that reported very deliberate and carefully calculated fraudulent tabulations of traffic flow counts for Highway 23. This week we have the distinction of being the first paper to report that last week's report was wrong.

We have learned of a farmer in Iowa County who claimed that he got $10 from the Republicans to vote a straight Republican ticket. He also said that he got $15 from the Democrats to vote a straight Democratic ticket. When questioned further he said, "I decided to vote for the Republicans because they were less corrupt."

Baseball is the only sport where, if you're on offense, the other team gets the ball. We feel that this isn't fair. We'd like to hear from you.

My neighbor was showing his son how to use his brand new bat and ball. He said, "Watch this very closely." Then he held the bat on his shoulder with one hand, and he flipped the ball into the air with the other hand. When the ball came down, he would take massive swings at it with the bat. The big problem was that he never once hit the ball, and his kid nearly caught pneumonia from the wind that was being generated by the bat.

In total awe, his kid said, "Dad, you're really a great pitcher."

I remember when I was just a little kid. My parents would try to teach me things. They spent about five years teaching me how to walk and talk, and then they sent me to school, where the only thing the teacher wanted me to do was sit down and shut up.

We had a very big family, and it seemed that somebody was always sick. There was constant sickness at our house, no matter what my parents did. For example, during flu season my dad bought one of those sanitary cups, and eventually we all got the flu, even though everybody used it.

CAMPING TIP: "How To Keep The Bears Away From Your Food."

Campers can purchase a small supply of any white chalky type powder, and use it to draw a large circular "end-zone" around their campsite.

A guy finds a very old brass oil lamp that has washed up onto a beach. When he brushes it off with a rag, a genie appears from within the lamp. The genie says, "I have truly great powers, and I'm used to doing things on a very grand scale. To a genie, a million years is but a moment, and a million dollars is very insignificant. I grant you any three wishes."

The guy is overwhelmed by all of this. He says, "This is really great. For my first wish I would like to have a million dollars."

The genie says, "No problem. Just make yourself comfortable while I do the paper work. It won't take but a moment."

Q. How do you get three little old ladies to grumble cuss words?
A. Have the fourth one yell, "Bingo."

A small puppy follows a young boy home. The boy asks, "Can I keep it?"

His mother says, "No. You can either find its owner and give it back, or you can give it to someone whose mother will let them have a puppy."

The kid leaves with the puppy. He is gone for quite a while. When he returns, he says, "Guess what? I sold the puppy for thirty dollars."

His mother says, "That's great. You can put the money in your bank."

The kid explains, "Well, it wasn't that kind of deal. I traded it for three, ten-dollar kittens."

We call our dog "Handy-man" because he does odd jobs around the house.

My neighbor rented the video "The King And I." He put it into his VCR, and watched the thing for about twenty minutes before he realized that it has nothing to do with Elvis.

One time he told me, "I need to borrow fifty bucks, but I have a hunch that you won't lend it to me."

I told him, "If I had hunches that were that accurate, I'd spend all my time at the track, betting on the horses."

Is he something or what? Sometimes when his wife is feeling really low, she will get out the old 8mm projector and the film from their wedding. To cheer herself up she runs the film backwards, and can watch herself backing down the aisle and out of the church, a free woman.

A young marine special forces recruit is being reprimanded for missing the last class in camouflage training. His reply: "I was there!"

Some newlyweds have moved into a house in the next block. It's cute. They are really in love. He takes the garbage out and she goes with him.

OVERHEARD AT THE SUPERMARKET:
"I remember when and where I got married. I just don't remember why."

Remember when people who wore blue jeans worked?

There was some rather serious flooding where my neighbor's group was hunting. They were stranded up in a tree for nearly six hours. When help arrived, the rescuers called from the boat, "We're from the Red Cross."
He called back, "I gave at the office."

Fortunately there is not much of anything in that part of the country, and the population is not very dense...with the obvious exception of my neighbor.

If opportunity knocked on his door, he would complain about the noise.

Golfer to caddy: "You've got to be the world's worst caddy."
Caddy to golfer: "No way. That would be too much of a coincidence."

To the list of things that smoking causes, you can add: Reports.

COMING NEXT WEEK:
Our detailed, nonpartisan and unbiased analysis of the ridiculous new budget strategies proposed by the Clinton Administration.

Merchant to farmer: "I'm afraid that I can't give you any more credit because your bill is bigger than it should be."
Farmer to merchant: "All right. Just reduce my bill to what it should be, and I'll pay it."

My wife thinks she bowls better than she golfs because, when she bowls, she never loses any balls.

It was a warm, sunny spring day. Two old gents were outside sitting on the porch when a very attractive young woman walked by. Once she passed, one old-timer looked at the other and said, "At times like this I kind of wish I was eighty again."

Nearsighted bank robber: "Everyone put your hands up...Are they up?"

Last summer I bought a sundial for our yard. When I was setting it up, my neighbor came over and asked, "What's that for?"

I explained, "The sun hits that small triangular spike that's sticking up from the center, and casts a shadow into the face of the sundial. Then, as the sun moves across the sky, the shadow also moves across the calibrated dial, enabling a person to determine the correct local time."

He shook his head and said, "What will they think of next?"

Is he a beauty! One time he wrecked their car, and the insurance agent came over to settle the claim. He asked, "How much money will we get?"

The agent said, "We don't give you any money. We replace your old car with another one just like it."

His wife thought about that for awhile and then said, "Well, if that's the way you people work, you can cancel the policy on my husband."

He wanted to borrow fifty bucks from me. I said, "Lending money to a friend is one sure way to ruin a friendship."

He said, "As far as I'm concerned, we're not all that close."

OUR THOUGHT FOR THE DAY: "A barking dog never bites... while barking."

A guy arrives at the gates of Heaven. Saint Peter says, "In checking our records I find that you have never done anything outstanding enough to get you into Heaven."

The guy says, "What about when I came to the aid of the little old man who was being pushed around by those thugs from that motor-cycle gang?"

Obviously impressed, Saint Peter looks through the record books again. Finding nothing, he says, "You did that?"

The guy says, "Yes. I kicked over a couple of the bikes and told them to pick on someone their own size."

Saint Peter is puzzled. He says, "There is absolutely no record of it. When did it happen?"

The guy says, "About ten minutes ago."

Q. "What's the difference between outlaws and in-laws?"

A. "Outlaws are wanted."

LETTER FROM A READER:

"Correct me if I'm wrong, but it appears to me that you are printing the same news every week. The only thing that seems to change is that it happens to different people."

The first farm wife says, "I was really embarrassed. We were out to eat at this very nice restaurant and my husband starts loudly talking about how much manure he has to spread. When we're in public like that, the least he could do is call it fertilizer."

The second one says, "I can't even get my husband to call it manure."

TWO NEIGHBOR LADIES TALKING:

"My husband is a big grouch. Is your husband hard to please?"

"I'm not sure. I've never tried."

Grandma could hardly be labeled a feminist. On the other hand, she isn't against pointing out that Ginger Rogers did everything Fred Astaire did, only Ginger Rogers had to do it going backwards and wearing high heels.

OUR THOUGHT FOR THE DAY:

Ego is the only thing that can keep on growing without nourishment.

A week ago I was in the resort town of Coeur d'Alene, Idaho. I decided to stop for lunch. An elderly couple sitting near me was having a bit of an argument about how to pronounce "Coeur d'Alene." Trying to settle the argument, they stopped a high-school-age boy who was cleaning up tables. They said, "Please, very slowly, tell us where we are." The kid said, "Bur...ger...King."

If you believe the famous General Douglas MacArthur line that suggests: "Old soldiers just fade away," try getting into your old uniform again.

When you are too heavy and trying to lose some weight, they recommend: "Eat slowly, and you will eat less." If you are like me, and come from a big family with many hungry mouths competing for the food, you remember that this was also true even when you weren't trying to lose weight.

Speaking of being overweight. My neighbor recently returned a necktie because it was too tight.

What a guy! He was reading that the vast majority of traffic accidents happen within ten miles of home, so he's considering moving.

It doesn't make any difference to me, but how many people do you think actually keep their gloves in the glove compartment?

Soviet farmers used to think twice before telling secrets on the farm. Their feeling was: "Potatoes have eyes, corn has ears and beans talk."

For whatever it is worth, I still don't understand her, but I'm pretty sure that my wife thinks: "If you charge it, it won't cost you anything, and if you put a cherry in it, it's less intoxicating."

THOUGHT FOR THE DAY:
While card playing can certainly be risky, it's not the only risky game that begins by holding hands.

A guy who came to the United States from Italy worked for awhile in an Italian restaurant. Before too long he applied for U.S. citizenship. One of the questions asked was, "Who is the new president?"
The applicant answered, "That'sa Mister Bill Clinton."
Next they asked, "Could you become the president?"
The applicant said, "No. That'sa not possible."

They asked, "Why not?"

He said, "I gotta way too mucha to do at the restaurant."

———

I realize now that I never set any high goals for myself. For example, as a little kid, my dream was that: "Some day I would grow up and become the Vice President."

———

OVERHEARD ON AN AIRLINER:

"I wish they'd just leave that stupid seat belt sign off. Every time they turn it on it gets bumpy."

———

My uncle wasn't a smoker. He chewed tobacco. In fact, he was absolutely the sloppiest tobacco chewer I have ever seen. Eventually it killed him. He got cancer of the chin.

———

CORRECTION: Last month I offered some bad advice to a reader who wrote because he wasn't getting along with his wife. I regret that there was a typo in the reply. I accidentally used the word FAKE. It should have read "Try to TAKE an interest in your wife's problems and concerns."

———

These days the marriages just do not last very long. In fact, any more, if I write a check for a wedding gift, I postdate it.

———

However, one couple I know got divorced, and then they got re-married. They said, "The divorce didn't work."

———

During an election year there are speeches in the air, and vice versa.

———

I have found a rather simple, yet fairly reliable method to estimate the cost of living. You just take your income, and add ten percent.

———

A politician is being questioned during a "John Doe" investigation:

"Did you receive money or favors from any lobbyists two years ago?"

"That's an insult. I won't legitimatize that question with an answer."

"Did you receive any money or favors from any lobbyists last year?"

"This is outrageous. I refuse to answer that question as well."

"Did you receive money or favors from any lobbyists so far this year?"

"No."

During the jury selection the prosecuting attorney poses the question: "Have you ever taken a bribe to fix the outcome of a court case?"

For several seconds there is no response, so the judge looks over at the potential juror and says, "Will you please answer the question?"

The guy says, "I'm sorry, your honor. I thought he was talking to you."

MODERN WEDDING VOW:
"I take thee, John, to be my lawfully wedded first husband."

My wife's on some kind of exotic health food kick. I'm afraid to find out what we're gonna have for dinner. She told me to stop on my way home and pick up some apple stems.

In a restaurant in New York City, I was approached by a guy who asked, "You wanna buy a gold watch?"

I said, "Maybe, and maybe not. Where is it?"

He said, "Shhh. Right now, the guy in the next booth is wearing it."

When I was a kid, I'd practice golf out in the pasture behind the barn. That's where I perfected my chip shot.

I always called a spade a spade, until I tripped over one in the dark.

ONE GOLFER TO ANOTHER:
"I'm not gonna play golf with Roger anymore. He cheats."

"What do you mean?"

"He lost a ball and then claimed he found it two feet from the green."

"That's possible."

"It isn't if I had the ball in my pocket."

Whoever suggested that golf is a game for rich people was dead wrong. There are an unbelievable number of poor players.

Congress continues to debate whether or not out-of-control spending is this nation's number one problem. Well, I can assure you that it is not. Our number one problem is listening to that out-of-control Congress.

Another problem we have in this country is the number of people trying to get something for nothing...and all of the government funded programs that enable them to succeed.

Monologue: A conversation between a person who's just had an operation and another who hasn't.

My neighbor's entire operation took only fifteen minutes, and it takes him DAYS to tell you about it.

Even though his operation was an out-patient procedure he says that it was a very serious thing. He says, "I'm just glad that I did not have to spend several days in the expensive care ward."

Talk about creative use of words. One of my favorites is: FERNANCER." As in, "He won't take no fernancer."

Our thought for the day involves those visits from unexpected company. REMEMBER: "The smaller the drink, the shorter the visit."

Modern medicine has increased our life expectancy to the point that it makes a lot of sense to worry about passing on an enormous national debt to our children. We may live long enough to have to pay it ourselves.

There's too much violence, tension and stress in the world these days. I finally decided to turn off the six o'clock news and work on my taxes, just to unwind.

So much clothing is being bought from mail-order catalogs these days. You'd think the post offices could at least provide some fitting rooms.

I noticed that my wife was watching some television show Monday night. Everyone was wearing wrinkled suits and T-shirts. Nobody wore any socks. It appeared as if they hadn't shaved for several days. I thought it was a special about the homeless. Turns out it was a *Miami Vice* re-run.

Speaking of being poorly dressed...my neighbor was late for work again the other morning. In his hurry to dress, he somehow missed every one of the belt loops on his pants. He was outside heading for his car when he found it impossible to take large steps.

I didn't realize way how bow-legged he is until I saw him standing there with his pants around his ankles, looking like a giant pair of pliers.

This guy's got more problems than a Yugo. He also has chronic insomnia and he is dyslexic. His wife says that he stays up all night wondering if there is really a dog.

He was taking shots for a cold, until his wife hid the bottle.

Q. "How can you tell if a car is from California?"
A. "Instead of a license plate in front, there's a pedestrian."

OVERHEARD ON CHRISTMAS MORNING:
"It's just what I've always wanted. Did you keep the sales slip?"

I read a newspaper story that claimed that there are ninety-seven deer pulling Santa's sleigh, and the figures were supposedly well documented. They were counted by the DNR.

Last month my neighbor wanted to sell his car. He took a magic marker and printed a sign reading: "For Sale By Owner" and taped it on his car. It's kinda picky, but the words "By Owner" bother me. I mean...who else?

Here's a beauty. One time he called the Better Business Bureau trying to find out when business was going to get better.

Sometimes, in his own way, my neighbor is kind of sharp. One time when he was in New York a guy said, "Hey! You see that big bridge over there? That is the very famous Brooklyn Bridge. I happen to be the owner, and I am willing to sell it very cheap. You wanna buy it?"

My neighbor asked, "How much?"

The guy said, "Two hundred dollars."

My neighbor said, "Really? That's a very fair price. Let me use your pen and I'll write you a check."

When the dealing was over his wife said, "What on earth are you doing? You known darn well that he does not own that stupid bridge, and you also know the bank closed your checking account. Neither of you got anything. You're both idiots. This whole thing was a big waste of everybody's time."

My neighbor said, "I got his pen."

What I hate is that my wife constantly compares me with him. She says, "The best part about being a man is that you don't have to marry one."

OUR THOUGHT FOR THE DAY: Absolutely nobody should be allowed to play an electric guitar until he knows how.

WOMAN TO WOMAN:

"Working full-time and trying to do the housework too, really gets me. After work I came home and I washed the clothes and I washed the dishes. Tomorrow I have to wash the kitchen floor and wash the front windows..."

"What about your husband?"

"Absolutely not! He can wash himself."

While the bathtub was invented in the year 1850, the telephone was not invented until the year 1875. Simple subtraction is all that's needed to figure out that, in the year 1850, a person could have spent 25 years in the bathtub, and never once have the telephone ring.

You're wondering, "Where did people bathe before there were bathtubs?" If they were lucky, their land had a spring on it, and they

133

would bathe in the spring. In fact, that's not only where they were likely to bathe, that's also when.

Years ago there were a lot of large families. This wasn't an accident. They figured, with a large family, there's a better chance that at least one of the kids wouldn't turn out like the others.

OVERHEARD IN A CARD GAME:
"I didn't say that you were cheating. I merely said that the top card looked kinda dusty."

Manager: "Do as I say and you could be the next world's champion."
Boxer: "I was more interested in being THIS WORLD'S champion."

Two can eat as cheap as one. Just ask the parents of a kid in college.

There are some signs that the economy is getting better, but we're not quite out of the woods yet.The other day I noticed that, along with all their "KEEP OFF THE GRASS" signs, the hardware store still stocks a big bunch of "DON'T EAT THE GRASS" signs.

There was loud, shrill screeching as he pulled the bow back and forth over the strings of his violin. This caused the dog to start in wailing. After several minutes of the duet, the kid's father hollered to his wife, "It's bad enough he has to practice while I'm trying to read the paper, but can't he at least play something the dog doesn't know?"

SIGN OUTSIDE A CHURCH:
"Competing with area businesses is getting tougher. We merely ask that you keep in mind...we were the first to be open on Sundays."

There is truth in advertising, even in the used car industry. A couple years ago I bought a used car. One of the big selling points was that it had factory air. No doubt about it. It did. Odors, fumes, smoke...

FRUSTRATED DRIVING INSTRUCTOR TO TRAINEE:
"Well, we still have a few minutes left. I think I should show you how to file an accident report."

DRIVING TIP: Always try to keep several car lengths between your car and the tree that may end up in front of you.

PARENTING TIP: When your kid says, "I'm sixteen now and I want to be treated like an adult," say, "Fine. Make the car payments."

My neighbor told me that he's strongly against the practice of tipping in hotels and restaurants. He says he is not alone either. There is an organization that was formed to try to abolish all tipping. They sent an application to him. When he found out that their membership fee was five dollars a year, he said, "It's cheaper for me to just keep on tipping."

What a guy! Last week he filed a complaint at the post office that he was getting threatening letters in the mail. As the postmaster took the complaint, he asked, "Do you have any idea who is sending these letters?"
My neighbor said, "Yes. The Internal Revenue Service."

The phone rang. My wife answered the kitchen phone at the very same time that I answered the front-room phone. I heard her say, "Hello."
Then I heard the guy calling say, "Don't hold supper for me. I'm going to be late." He obviously didn't know he had dialed the wrong number.
My wife played right along with me when I motioned for her to hang up. This is terrible. I feel guilty, and wonder what he thought when I said, "That's fine with us. Just take your time." Then I hung up too.

The professor of an economics class asks, "If all the advertising for food products were to stop tomorrow, how many people would stop eating?"
A guy in the back says, "A whole bunch of advertising executives."

There really is truth in advertising. Last week I saw an advertisement for collapsible lawn chairs. I bought one. Sure enough, every time I sit in it...it does.

IN THE CLASSIFIED ADS:
Lost: A black cat with white paws. Answers to an electric can opener.

My neighbor was one of the people nominated for "Employee-of-the-year" at work last year. That'll give you some idea what kind of year it was.

One time he made the statement: "If I had money, I'd travel."
His wife couldn't resist asking, "How much would it take?"

He went to Vegas hoping to meet Lady Luck and ran into Miss Fortune.

While driving through the mountains of West Virginia, I stopped to get directions from an old-timer who was walking along the side of the road. We got to talking about living in the hills. I asked him if the cost of buying daily necessities has gone up there, like it has everywhere else.
He said, "It sure enough has. And even if you got the money to buy it, the stuff usually ain't fit to drink."

I can't believe the doctors at the local veterinary clinic. I stopped there and asked, "Do you have anything that will cure fleas?"
They said, "We might. Do you have any idea what made them sick?"

ET CETERA [etc.]: A term that's used to make people think we know more about something than we really do.

My wife wanted a better car for Christmas, but I got her some pearls. Would have gotten her a car, but they don't make imitation cars.

Last month my neighbor sold an old car to his brother-in-law for $200. His brother-in-law gave it a good wash job, and when my neighbor saw it, it looked so good he offered to buy it back for $250. His brother-in-law took the money and gave the car back to him. Then his brother-in-law got to thinking he should have kept the car. In fact, it bothered him so badly, he stopped over at my neighbor's house and offered him $350 for the car. My neighbor saw an opportunity for a quick profit, so he sold it back to his brother-in-law.

As you have probably already guessed, my neighbor got to thinking that his brother-in-law must know something about this car, that he doesn't. Before very long he is absolutely certain that he sold the car too cheap and he offers his brother-in-law $400 to buy the car back.

Here's where it gets good. His brother-in-law tells him that he's sold the car to a friend of his at work. My neighbor says, "You sold it to an outsider? What a dope! We had a real good thing with just the two of us. We both were making a very nice profit on a regular basis."

I saw him out on the golf course, teeing off from a spot that was well in front of the mark. I said, "Hey, you cheater. Go back behind the line." He sheepishly looked around to see who else may have heard the comment. Then he said, "Will you shut up? This is my second stroke."

It turns out that the winner of the New York City Marathon wasn't even registered in the race. He was just a tourist who thought that all those other people were muggers who were after him.

The personnel director asks, "Why do you want a job with our company?"

The job applicant explains, "I was sick, and I went to see the doctor. He gave me these pills and said that I should take one after every meal. That was two weeks ago, and I've still got a bunch of pills left."

OVERHEARD DURING COFFEE BREAK:

"Every night when we watch television my husband makes such a big fuss that I've decided to just let him pick out everything we watch."

"Does that keep him happy?"

"I don't do it to keep him happy. I did it to keep him quiet."

MODERN MARRIAGE TRENDS:
Shorter honeymoons, but more of them.

A young bride tells her mother, "My Bill talks in his sleep all night, and it's so bad that I don't get any sleep. What should I do?"
Her mother says, "Give him more chances to talk during the day."

My wife gets mad at me for the least little thing. She got mad because I was talking in the movie theater last week. I wasn't actually talking. All I did was tell her that there was some chewing gum under my seat.
She said, "You are absolutely disgusting. Shut-up and watch the show."
Then, I guess, I really got her mad when I said, "Yuk! It's Spearmint."

For me, the hardest part about being an adult is acting like one.

At home my disposition is very sweet, but my wife is extremely grumpy. Now I believe I know why. There's an old saying: "You are what you eat." Every morning at breakfast, I'll have a couple of sweet rolls and coffee with three or four lumps of sugar in it. But my wife starts her day off with a cup of vinegar poured over a big bowl of carpet tacks.

In the coat room of this little restaurant where I'd just eaten lunch, some guy came up to me and said, "Are you Ernie Olson from Minneapolis?"
I said, "No."
He said, "Well, I am, and that's his coat you're putting on."

A while back I read a human interest type news item from the paper to my wife. I said, "It says here that only one woman in ten can whistle."
She said, "That's probably because only one man in ten is worth it."

I also read that researchers have now come up with another new theory. The latest one is that people who have an active love life are also more prone to have a good memory. I'm not making this up. I actually read it. I don't remember where I read it, but I swear that's what it said.

OVERHEARD IN A BARBERSHOP:
"In the Old West they didn't pamper criminals. They put horse thieves in jail for a month, on nothing but bread and water."
"I bet they'd never steal another horse."
"No, they didn't steal any more horses, because after a month in jail on nothing but bread and water, they'd hang 'em."

I don't watch much television. Just enough to notice that on television, the good guys win everywhere, except on the six o'clock news.

I now know why so many women spend so much time watching those daytime television soap operas. Yesterday I watched one. Through the entire show the wife has an affair with another man, and then at the end of the show the husband begs for forgiveness.

OVERHEARD AT THE DINNER TABLE:
"Did I mention that I got a parking ticket today?"
"No. Where did you park?"
"They'll go over those details in court. I guess I was double parked."
"Okay...where did you double park?"
"On top of this other car."

A New York cab driver jams the brakes on to avoid hitting a pedestrian. He turns around and explains to his passenger, "If you hit them, you have to fill out a report."

A teacher took her class on a bus trip to visit the Statue of Liberty. During their ride home she attempts to test their powers of observation. She asks, "Who knows which hand the statue was holding in the air?"
From the back of the bus a kid yells, "The one with the torch."

Marriage Ball: Your wife gets mad and throws a fit, and you catch it.

In a bait shop, a guy about to go fishing is considering some minnows. He asks the manager, "Do you think these minnows are any good?"

The manager says, "I don't, but the fish do."

An actor goes to see his psychiatrist. He says, "I think I'm getting an inferiority complex. I'm beginning to think there are other people who are just as good as I am."

A rich old lady gets a big box of chocolate from an unemployed nephew. A week later he calls and asks, "How'd my favorite aunt like the candy?" She says, "To tell you the truth, I haven't been able to try them yet. They're still at the chemist's."

POEM: [Anonymous]

One day in late October
I was far from being sober
After taking on a load of manly pride.
My feet began to stutter
And I fell into the gutter
When a pig came up and lay down by my side.
As I lay there in gutter
Thinking thoughts I dare not utter
A lady passing by was heard to say,
"You can tell a man who boozes
By the company he chooses."
And the pig got up and slowly walked away.

SIGN IN A DIVORCE LAWYER'S OFFICE:
"Satisfaction guaranteed or your honey back."

In some cultures marriages are arranged by community marriage brokers. In one such community a couple is approached by the marriage broker with a very surprising proposal. The marriage broker asks for the approval of a marriage of their forty-year-old son. Their son has zero personality. He is short, pudgy and balding. And, as if that isn't enough, he's never been able to keep either a job or a girlfriend.

Their consent is needed for him to marry a beautiful young woman who is highly intelligent and recent heir to a multi-million dollar estate.

The mother says, "It doesn't make much sense to me, but I'll certainly give my consent."

The father says, "You have my consent too."

140

The marriage broker says, "That's wonderful. I'll be back just as soon as I can. Now I've got to see if I can get the young woman to consent."

At a big Texas barbecue party, a social climbing guest confronts an extremely wealthy Texas rancher with the following classic line:
"I'm not sure if we've ever met. How much did you say your name was?"

My neighbor was telling me that he was warned: "If you want to survive, you'll have to give up drinking, gambling and womanizing."
I told him, "You'd better do what the doctor says."
He said, "What doctor? The warning was from my accountant."

There are bigger things in life than money. In his case they're bills.

SIGN IN OPTOMETRIST'S WINDOW:
"If you don't see what you want, you've come to the right place."

They say: "Time is the great healer." That's probably why they always make you wait so long in the doctor's office.

Not all women are guilty of repeating gossip. Some of them start it.

The economy being what it is these days, the minister consoles the congregation: "Remember, there will be no buying or selling in Heaven."
A guy in the back of church grumbles to his wife, "I'm not surprised. That's not where business has gone."

The phrase: "Close to public transportation" is a real estate term that probably means the house is located about two hundred yards off the end of runway 32L at Chicago's O'Hare Field.

The teacher asks the children to be quiet, but it doesn't do any good. After a second request brings no noticeable results, she is rather upset. She hollers, "I'm not going to start class until this room is so quiet you can hear a pin drop."

Little by little the kids begin to quiet down, and eventually the room is totally quiet. Then from the back of the room some smart-aleck yells, "Okay, let 'er drop!"

The teacher asks, "What distinguishes George Washington from all of the other presidents?" Immediately several kids respond, "He didn't lie."

My neighbor and his wife are fighting again. He promised that, after his lodge meeting was over, he would have one drink and be home by ten. He got all confused. He had ten drinks and got home at one.

One time he told her that he took their son to the zoo. She believed him until the kid told her that one of the animals paid twenty-to-one.

He's got more problems than a two dollar watch. A while ago he stepped on a rake and the handle came up and hit him on the head. But he's okay. He said that he went to a doctor who took a bunch of X-rays of his head that showed nothing.

When he registered for the draft, he was rated 4E. He thought it was a typo, but they said the "E" was correct. They said it stands for "Even." He said, "Even what?" They said, "Even if we get invaded, don't come."

I always wondered why so many people moved south when they grew older. Now I am old enough to see that it's all dictated by gravity. As you age, so much of your body starts to slide south anyway, you might just as well go with the flow.

I'm now at the age where I'm still ready, willing and able, but seldom all three at the same time.

My wife doesn't seem to be aging as fast as me. Or at least if she is, it's had no affect on her memory. She vividly, and regularly, remembers every mistake I've ever made.

Making a mistake in front of my wife is like cutting yourself in front of Dracula.

SIGN ON THE WALL OF A GALLEY SHIP:
"The beatings will continue until the morale improves."

Congress has always been a little bit jealous that "Hail to the Chief" is traditionally played when a President enters the room. It seems to me that this petty jealousy would be pretty much eliminated if Congress had its own song. I'd like to suggest "Send in the Clowns."

And then there's the Australian inventor whose first invention involved combining a hand grenade with a boomerang. It was also his last.

Some salesman was over at my neighbor's house trying to sell him a set of encyclopedias. The guy said, "An encyclopedia is great if you've got kids that go to school."
My neighbor said, "They can walk to school just like I did."

One time his wife got him a watch that was waterproof, shockproof, and it also had an unbreakable crystal. He lost it.

REMEMBER: In backwards countries you shouldn't drink the water, and in industrialized countries you shouldn't breath the air.

I think that I've figured out why my wife is so crazy about Chinese food. Won Ton spelled backwards is: "Not now."

My uncle golfs with some guys that take it too seriously. One time he had a stroke while they were golfing, and they made him count it.

Speaking of golf...I have my golf socks on today. There's a hole in one.

When I was a kid my socks had so many holes in them, I could put them on from either end.

We were poor. Mom would give us stale bread and tell us it was toast.

Times were tough back then. There were five of us sleeping in one bed, until my oldest brother got married. Then there were six.

I remember Mom telling me, "It doesn't matter if you are rich or poor. In this country anyone can grow up and become a taxpayer."

When I was in school, I was always very proud of the fact that I could do something that nobody else could do. Read my handwriting.

The only thing I know about sailing is that port is red.

The Indy 500 race is over for another year, and for all those who were involved in it, the pressure was overwhelming. Every racer realizes that no matter how hard you try, no matter how much you spend, no matter what you do, the fact remains that, out of all the cars in the field only one is a winner. On the other hand, those are a lot better odds than you get on a used car lot.

If you think about it, winning is not a big deal. To win at something, you have to beat somebody who is not as good. Anybody can do that.

Relative to my driving abilities...Call me careless. Call me reckless. However, making one lousy right turn from the left lane doesn't make me what the guy behind me called me.

Frustration: A live secret and a dead telephone.

Wild horses couldn't drag a secret out of my wife. The big problem is she doesn't have lunch with wild horses.

Want people to believe what you say? Try this. Before speaking, pause. Then glance to your left and glance to your right. Then whisper it.

The problem with antique shops is that everything is from the old days except the prices.

During survival training a new army recruit is given a bucket and sent down to the river to get some fresh water. He's in the water for a short time when he runs back yelling, "There's an alligator in the water."

The sergeant says, "Soldier, that alligator is much more afraid of you than you are of it."

The recruit says, "In that case, that water ain't fit to drink."

Our survey is over. Results show that taxpayers are alive and kicking.

Those surveyed said they were aware that money does not grow on trees, but by the time they realized it, they were already way out on a limb.

Obesity was another widespread concern. In summary, most people stated: "If only we retained as much of what we earn, as we do of what we eat."

For "Best Parody of A Phrase From An Obnoxious TV Commercial" the vote went to: "Help, I'm talking and I can't shut up."

I try to see the brighter side of things. I lay awake nights thinking, "At least my problems haven't given me insomnia."

My neighbor's got problems. He caused another big dispute. His doctor wants him to take up golf, and the club pro wants him to give it up.

For their silver wedding anniversary his wife wants a huge celebration. She wants to celebrate that the first twenty-five years of the marriage are finally over.

A rich woman was very proud of the vase that she bought at an auction. She decides to hire a painter to paint her bedroom walls the exact color of the vase. She offers to pay any painter well, if he can exactly match the vase. A few painters try. Each uses his very own special mixing, and blending methods. Each comes close, but when the paint dries, none comes close enough to satisfy the eccentric woman. The woman becomes obsessed, and offers a huge sum of money to anyone who can exactly match the vase.

Eventually she gets contacted by a painter who claims that he can make it match exactly. And he does. Word gets out. The painter becomes famous but he never reveals the method he used to get the exact match.

The day finally comes when he decides to retire and turn the business over to his son. The son says, "Dad, there is something I've gotta know. How did you get those walls to match the vase so perfectly?"

The father says, "I also painted the vase."

We've had more than enough of this rainy, humid weather. At our house, one of the things that was starting to mildew was a bottle of bleach.

There is no way anyone is going to believe this, but I'm going to tell it anyway so people realize just how soggy the fields are. I was driving on a back road, and I noticed a cap laying in a muddy field. This is not a joke. Then I saw the cap rise and I saw that it was on someone's head. The head belonged to the farmer who owned the field. I figured he walked into the field not realizing how deep the mud was. There was no way that I could reach him because it was so muddy, so I threw a rope out to him.

He grabbed the rope; then he sank totally out of sight. So I pulled on the rope, and he came back up and yelled, "Don't pull, I'm not ready."

I yelled, "Hold on." But he didn't hear because he went under again.

I pulled again, and he surfaced once more and yelled, "Don't pull yet. I'm not ready."

I couldn't believe it. I said, "What are you doing? Just hang on!"

He said, "I'm trying to tie the rope to the front of my tractor."

CORRECTION: The lunch listed in the School Lunch Menu section of last week's paper should have read, "ground hog meat" not "groundhog meat."

146

SPECIALIST: A doctor who has a smaller practice, but a larger house.

Speaking of specialists, my neighbor said his great, great grandfather was a "Pre-cognitive, Equestrian Location Specialist." That means that he would find lost horses before they were lost.

He was telling me that, in the 1830's, his ancestors came to this area in covered wagons. He even pulled out their old family album, and showed me some photographs of his ancestors. After seeing the pictures of them, I can fully understand why they covered the wagons.

I was at the counter checking out, and commented to the guy behind me, "Can you believe this? I just spent eighty-seven bucks on groceries, and look how small the bag is."
The check-out clerk said, "You want a bigger bag?"

Nobody takes me seriously. A few days ago I stopped at the veterinary clinic and asked what they'd recommend for fleas. They said, "A dog."

My uncle got a big surprise in the mail. Someone sent two tickets to a baseball game and a note that read: "You'll never guess who sent these." The seats weren't so good, but that didn't matter because he and my aunt spent the entire game trying to figure out who sent the tickets.
Then they got home and found that all of their valuables were missing, and there was another note saying, "Now you know."

The boss says, "Every time I come into your office you're goofing off. I'd like to know why."
The employee says, "You don't knock."

"Waitress, in your ad it says that you blend your own coffee, but this doesn't taste like blended coffee."
"Well, it is. It's a blend of yesterday's and this morning's."

My neighbor and his wife went out to eat at a rather fancy restaurant. He pointed to the "Escargot" on the menu and asked,

"What's that?" She said, "Don't you know? That's French. Those are snails." He said, "How would I know? I normally only eat fast food."

This is the same guy who says that he doesn't need to use toothpaste, because his teeth aren't loose.

OUR THOUGHT FOR THE DAY:
"A bird in the hand is worth two in the bush...unless you're a bird."

A guy that is being considered for possible jury duty stands and says, "Your honor, I know the defendant is guilty. Look at those shifty eyes."
The judge says, "Would you please sit down. That is not the defendant. That's his lawyer."

TWO TRUCKERS OVERHEARD AT A TRUCK STOP:
"It looks like rain."
"I guess it does, but at least it smells like coffee."

In the early days of medicine, doctors would regularly bleed patients who came to them with ailments. In a manner of speaking they still do.

I felt I needed to lose a few pounds, so I bought some reducing pills. The only thing I lost was the price of the pills.

After several days on the mountain, Moses comes down and announces to the waiting crowd, "I've got good news. We will not have to obey sixteen commandments after all. I talked with God, and I was able to get it down to just ten commandments. Unfortunately, adultery is still one of them."

My neighbor was saying, whenever he and his wife get into an argument, right away she gets historical. I said, "You mean hysterical?"
He said, "I mean historical. She recalls everything I ever did wrong, and the exact day, date and time that it happened."

My wife and I had "words" the other day. It was just a little flare-up that was ignited when she caught me talking with an old flame.

I never got into trouble when I chased women. My problems didn't start until I caught one.

During my younger days I subscribed to the theory of male superiority. Then I got married, and my wife cancelled my subscription.

A few days ago, while his wife was pointing out some things she wanted him to repair on the front of the house, my neighbor snuck out the back and went fishing. But he didn't catch anything...until he got home.

I guess I'm just getting old. Any more I don't care where my wife goes as long as I don't have to go along.

We had to get married. I couldn't afford to keep taking her out.

The money I made used to talk turkey. Lately it isn't saying beans.

We still go out once in awhile, but always to the "fast food" places. For us, a fancy restaurant is any place where your beverage doesn't have a plastic lid, and the table has four legs.

You know what bothers me most? Whenever my wife and I do go somewhere, we're usually late, because she takes so long to get ready. And if we're not late, it's because she lost track of the time.

We argue about this and a bunch of other things, but when her mind is made up, nothing can change it. I realize some people have closed minds, but my wife's mind is hermetically sealed.

She is FAST! She makes up her mind the moment I voice an opinion.

I'm not being picky. I really believe that the reason we argue so much is because we somehow ended up with a bed that has two wrong sides.

We each have different philosophies regarding taking a vacation. I'm the kind who wants to get away from it all. She's the kind who wants to pack it all.

A few times, when my gas gauge was on empty, and I wasn't sure I'd get to the next gas station, I'd lean forward. The more that needle dropped, the more I'd lean. I knew that leaning wouldn't help. On the other hand, I never ran out of gas, so apparently, it also doesn't hurt. [FYI]

My doctor told me that it's very healthy to walk, but I'm not so sure. I've never seen a mailman who looked like he could whip a truck driver.

Most accidents happen in the kitchen, but I don't complain. I just use a lot of ketchup, and eat whatever it is on the plate.

On the brighter side...I think I have finally broken the stupid dog of begging for food from the table. I let her taste some.

I remember when she was just a young puppy, it was extremely difficult to get her to kick the rug habit.

I can sympathize with the dog, because when I was young I occasionally had a few little accidents too. They were excusable because I was young. Now that I'm older I have to come up with other excuses.

Mrs. Tooey gave birth to twin baby boys. You couldn't tell them apart. One was the spitting image of the other...so she called him Hock.

This country is really in need of some politicians whose promises last at least as long as their bumper stickers.

At a luncheon [where I was hired to provide the laughs] I sat next to, and was constantly upstaged by, a very funny little old lady who was in her eighties. [This one is true.] At one point she showed us her pills, and the instructions which read: "Take one pill, three times a day."

She said, "How am I supposed to do that...tie a string to it?"

Two burglars had a rather close call recently. After breaking into the rear window of a house one night, they discovered that the guy who lived there was an insurance salesman. But they were very quiet and were able to sneak back out again without buying anything.

"Some people shouldn't wear stretch pants to a public shopping mall."

"Those aren't stretch pants. They just...don't have any other choice."

A little kid finds a stray dog in front of the house. His mother says, "Don't you dare bring that thing in the house. It's full of fleas."

The kid goes back out and tells the dog, "You can't come in the house. It's full of fleas."

Little Johnny runs home after his very first day in school. He grabs the newspaper and pages through it from front to back. Then he throws the paper down and walks away grumbling, "I STILL can't read!"

My neighbor says, "I like to enter those marathon runs because it shows that I can do something."

His wife says, "So does doing something."

He claims he's a workaholic. He's afraid if he ever takes another job, he won't be able to stop.

OVERHEARD AT A DANCE: "My boyfriend and I split up because we aren't compatible. I'm a Virgo and he's an idiot."

"Does your husband still find you exciting after all these years?"

"Not if I can help it."

A reporter from the local newspaper is interviewing an old man who has just turned one hundred years old. She questions him about the old days. Eventually she smiles and asks, "What do you think of the modern women?"

He says, "I haven't thought about women for almost a year."

———————

While the hangman slides the noose tight, he asks the condemned golfer, "Do you have any last requests?"

The guy says, "Yes. Can I have a couple practice swings?"

———————

Prisoners are most often on death row for years because our government keeps staying their execution. But there is a form of capital punishment they have no qualms about using. They don't mind taxing us to death.

———————

My neighbor was watching some talk show where the guest was an expert on crime statistics. The guy said: "Your car is most likely to be stolen while it's parked in front of your own house."

So now my neighbor parks his car in front of MY house.

———————

It's not easy to have a serious conversation with him. He's got a chip on his shoulder, and I think it's chip dip on the front of his shirt.

———————

The neighbors had another small dispute. They usually argue about money. He thinks $300 is a fair price for the kids.

———————

A while ago my wife made some salad using an old family recipe she got from her grandma. The recipe calls for onions, garlic, Limburger cheese, skunk cabbage and wilted lettuce.

Actually it starts as crisp, fresh lettuce, but once it's in the bowl, it has no other choice. [This stuff even wilts the Tupperware].

———————

Everything in the refrigerator tastes and smells like the salad unless she uses this industrial strength baking soda made by Arm & Jackhammer.

———————

This isn't a joke. That salad would give Pac Man indigestion.

———————

Every once in a while she also makes Chinese food. The main problem with her Chinese food is, an hour later you're still chewing.

———————

I usually sleep through anything, but take my advice. Never stay at a hotel if its marquee says: "Welcome, National Society of Hog Callers."

This one hurts. At a family picnic I overheard my sister ask her kids, "Would you kids like to go home with Uncle Ron?"
The kids shouted, "NO!"
My sister said, "Then you'd better behave."

Golfer: "Are you any good at finding lost balls?"
Caddie: "Yes, sir. I'm very good at that."
Golfer: "Okay, find one and let's get going."

I heard that my neighbor went to the country club for a round of golf. He got eighteen holes in. He played nine, and dug nine.

He claims that he only had a couple divots, but the club pro says that they moved less dirt when they dug the swimming pool.

There's now a portable TV so small that it fits in the palm of your hand. It even has a remote control. I suppose you put that in your other hand.

Fireproof: That's what you become when you have something on the boss.

Two guys are having lunch when the first guy sees a very good-looking young woman at another table. He says, "Wow! Did you see her?"
The second guy says, "Yea. I know her."
The first guy says, "I've got to meet her. What's she like?"
The second guy says, "Five kids."
The first guy says, "She's got five kids?"
The second guy says, "No. You do."

I read an article which claims infidelity is at an all time high. When I showed it to my wife, she said, "You would never get involved with another woman. You're too decent. You're too caring. You're too old."

Lawyers for the casino gambling lobby went to court and attempted to limit the use of the well known phrase: "Marriage is a gamble."

They claim that with all of the turmoil and tension that's associated with modern marriages, the phrase is ruining their image.

My wife and I just had another little argument. At some point she said, "I'm willing to admit that I told a few white lies, if you'll also admit that you told a few white lies."

I was kind of tired anyway, so I reluctantly agreed, but the whole time I'm thinking, "One of us is color blind."

There's way too much stress in my life . To get my mind off of all the tension, I started golfing. Some of the tension eased when I finally broke eighty, but I don't know what I'm going to do now. That's all the clubs I had.

I told the doctor that I couldn't relax. He said, "Force yourself."

Now the neighbor's kid bought an electric guitar, and this great big amp. This amplifier is just huge! When he turns it on, the street lights dim.

It sounds like he only knows how to turn it on, and also how to turn it up. Learning how to actually play the guitar does not seem to be a priority. Without the ability to play, there's just this "amplified incompetence."

Last night he turned it on, and he turned it up while I was eating my dinner. The noise put ripples in my soup. You should hear it. What am I saying?

If you live less than fifty miles away, you probably do.

He has to keep it in their garage. That killer amp doesn't fit through any other door. The noise in that garage can bend metal. If he's not careful, he will be the only kid to ever total his dad's car, without even driving it.

It is one thing to be a little inconsiderate, but this is the kind of kid who would go to the movies, and stick his chewing gum on TOP of a seat.

In this little town in Cuba an old man goes to the store every morning to buy a newspaper. He glances at the front page. Then he angrily throws the entire paper into the trash bin. Every morning it's the same thing.

One day the merchant asks, "Why do you buy the newspaper each morning, merely glance at the front page, and then throw the entire paper away?"

The man says, "I don't read it. I'm just looking for a death notice."

The merchant says, "In Cuban papers, death notices are in the back."

The man says, "Take my word for it. The death notice I am looking for will be on the front page."

Anyone who argues with his psychiatrist should have his head examined.

I tried jogging once. It didn't go too well. I got out of bed at 5 a.m., jogged a mile. By then it was noon.

The honeymoon is over. I asked my wife if she would close the curtains so the neighbors wouldn't see me running around in my underwear.

She said, "Don't worry. If any of the neighbors see you running around in your underwear, THEY will close the curtains."

The other day my neighbor and his wife had a discussion. She told him, "You snore really awful at night. No other man snores as bad as you do."

At first he denied it. Then he said, "Wait a minute. How do you know?"

She says, "I feel good all morning, and I feel great in the afternoon. But when I'm home at night, I feel lousy. Why do you suppose that is?"

My neighbor says, "How should I know?"

She tries again, "I feel good at work. Why do I feel so bad at home?"

He draws another blank. He says, "You got me."
She says, "Yup...that's the reason."

He feels he has a right to criticize, and she feels it's her duty.

Then there are those people who really seem to be made for each other. Take my grandparents. He snores. But she's hard of hearing.

The IRS called. They want to talk to me. I think it's about the letter I wrote to them. I may have gone too far. I vividly recall the last line. It said, "I can no longer afford your services."

Things could be worse. At least they don't charge for their tax forms.

I no longer worry about taxes. Something else is now the top priority. The never-ending television and newspaper ads have brought the new worry to my attention. I'm constantly reminded in the mail, and I get numerous telephone calls about it at my home. No doubt you have noticed this too. But if what they're saying is true, all of us are far too careless about which long distance telephone service we subscribe to.

Misery: An executive with an unlimited expense account and an ulcer.

Here's something that always puzzled me. Who was the first farmer to use manure to fertilize his crops? Even more bewildering, what on earth would have prompted him to even try it?

What really kills me is....it works!!

OVERHEARD AT A MOVIE THEATER:
"Can you see okay?"
"Yes."
"Do you feel a draft?"
"No."
"Is your seat comfortable?"

"It's just fine."

"Wanna trade?"

In a joke writing class one guy kept shouting out smart-aleck remarks. It got so bad that the professor decided he'd put this guy in his place. So he locked the guy in a closet, and told him that he wouldn't open it until the guy made a pun. The door was shut for only a few seconds when the class heard a knock on the door and a voice say, "O-pun the door."

Mechanics should offer two estimates. An estimate, and an estimate of how much more it will cost than the estimate.

The easiest way to raise rabbits is by not interfering.

The "How To" books have always sold well, but when it comes to romance you can learn a lot at the movies. That's assuming you're not distracted by the picture.

While I was watching a movie, a lovely young woman sat down in the seat next to me. Then she looked up at me and realized that she'd mistaken me for someone else. She said, "I'm sorry. I'm in the wrong seat."

I said, "It's the right seat. You're just twenty-five years too late."

Remember when an old fashioned couple was a couple who stayed married? These days it's a couple that gets married.

There's some good in everything. For example: If lawyers didn't charge substantially more to get divorced than the ministers do to get married, there would probably be even more divorces.

Only after they were married did my neighbor find out that his wife was a big spender...and she found out that he wasn't.

They met at a travel bureau. She was looking for something different, and he was. She says, "Some vacation. I ended up with the last resort."

Remember: The boss also watches the clock. The only difference is that the boss watches during coffee breaks.

A guy who was applying for a job brought in several reference letters. He had one letter from the pastor of his church. He had one letter from the assistant pastor of the church. He had two letters from two of the elders of the church.

The potential employer said, "These are really great, but can you get some from someone who knows you during the week?"

When golfing...nothing counts like the people you're playing with.

Three ways to get something done: Do it yourself. Hire someone else to do it. Forbid your kids to do it.

Up in the hills a census taker stops at a house and asks the woman how many people are living there.

She says, "Let's see. There's me and Pa. There's Billy-Bob, Sissy, and there's the twins, Ricky and Micky. There's Tommy and there's..."

The census taker stops her. He says, "I don't need names for a census. All I need is numbers."

She says, "We don't use numbers. We ain't run out of names yet."

The truth is normally clear as a bell, but it isn't always tolled.

You're going to think I'm making this up. A while back my neighbor was telling me that his entire body hurts. To demonstrate he took his finger and began to press on various parts of his body.

He poked his ribs and said, "This hurts." He pressed his arm and said, "Ouch! That hurts too." He pressed his foot and said, "It even hurts if I press down here on my foot."

I told him to see a doctor. He did. Turns out he had a broken finger.

On a recent cruise he spent much of his time leaning over the railing. His wife said, "I didn't know you had a weak stomach."

He said, "What do you mean weak? I'm heaving as far as everyone else."

One thing that is better to give than receive is a get-well card.

Just prior to the divorce he runs an ad saying: "I am not responsible for my wife's debts."
The very next day her attorney runs an ad saying: "We'll see."

OVERHEARD IN THE POST OFFICE:
"Whose picture is that on the wall?"
"It's some guy who is wanted by the government in Washington, D.C."
"What do they want him for?"
"He's a crook."
"Why would they want any more crooks in Washington, D .C.?"

The first grade teacher asks, "What is the shape of the earth?"
A kid in the back of the room yells, "Terrible."

I must have been a fast learner when I was a kid. I didn't have to join the Scouts to learn how to tie knots. All I needed was shoe laces.

The neighbor kid was crying. I asked, "What's wrong?"
He said, "My dad slipped and fell in a puddle of mud."
I said, "That's nothing to cry about. You should laugh at that."
He said, "I did."

One of the most dangerous ways to travel is via a wet bar of soap.

After my physical the doctor's recommendation was: "Take two aspirin, and a trip to Lourdes."

Chuck and Kathy are visited by Chuck's old army buddy who said that he can only stay the weekend. Ten days later he is still there, and he is driving them crazy. They don't know how to go about asking him to leave.
Chuck comes up with an idea. He says, "At dinner tonight I'll say that the food tastes funny. You say that it tastes fine. We'll pretend to

argue about it. Then I'll ask him for his opinion. If he sides with you, I'll ask him to leave, and if he sides with me, you ask him to leave."

That night at dinner Chuck says, "The food tastes funny."

Kathy says, "It tastes all right to me."

Then Chuck looks at his old army buddy and asks, "What do you think?"

His buddy says, "I've got no opinion. I want to stay one more week."

COUNTRY SONG TITLE:

"I'd Rather Have A Bottle In Front Of Me Than A Frontal Lobotomy."

She says, "Do you see that guy drinking all those martinis over at the bar? He's been drinking like that ever since I broke up with him."

Her friend says, "No way. He wouldn't celebrate that much."

HUSBAND ANSWERING THE PHONE:

"She's not at home. Would you like to leave a rumor?"

A woman is in front of the judge asking for a divorce. The judge says, "You've been married twenty years. Why do you want a divorce now?"

The woman says, "Because my husband has terrible table manners."

The judge says, "Why did you wait twenty years to ask for a divorce?"

The woman says, "I just bought the book last week."

When they married she said that she'd mend his ways. Now she realizes that he's not worth a darn.

Golfers are odd people. They shout "Fore," shoot six and mark five.

On the other hand, thanks to golfers and fishermen, sunbathers aren't the only ones who lie in the sun.

"Let me speak to the manager."

"He stepped out of the office for a while."

"Then let me speak to the assistant manager."

"He also stepped out of the office for awhile."

160

"Is the bookkeeper in?"

"Yes, but he's tied up right now."

"When will he be free?"

"Normally the managers untie him when they get back."

Attorneys' fees are now so high it's often cheaper to buy the judge.

I once tried to get a job with a carnival, but my teeth were too good.

I recently went to a strange wedding. Talk about tacky. The bride went to the altar with her hair up in rollers because she wanted to look nice for the reception.

At the reception they served Egg Foo Young. That in itself was weird, but they ran out of eggs, and then they ran out of young. By the time they served our table, all they had left was foo.

I should have known something was wrong because the head waitress kept looking the crowd over. The way she held her hand I couldn't tell if she was counting us, or blessing us.

If you want my opinion, I think the bride should have kept the bouquet and tossed the groom.

Speaking of shaky marriages. My neighbor recently won a trip for two to a ski resort, and his wife is irate. He went alone, twice.

He's not too graceful. I heard that on the slopes he had some rather unconventional moves. They say that he looked less like somebody skiing, and more like somebody being thrown out of a bar.

On the streets they say that the reason the Clintons are sending their daughter to a private school is because, if she went to a public school, the secret service would be out-gunned.

Government funded studies uncovered the reason old soldiers never die. It's because they make the young soldiers do all the fighting.

161

CORRECTION:
Last week's story about a Dodgeville man who made four million dollars in the lumber business was not totally correct. We have since learned it didn't happen in Dodgeville. It happened in Dallas. It wasn't the lumber business. It was the oil business. Also, it wasn't four million dollars. It was four hundred thousand dollars. And it was not the Dodgeville man. It was the Dodgeville man's brother. And he didn't make it. He lost it.

The main trouble with a farm is that, no matter where you are sitting, you're looking at something that needs doing.

Beware of all those politicians who keep promising you pie in the sky. They're going to use your dough.

The people of Wisconsin should stop all the capital punishment debating. It only confuses the issue. And just imagine how frustrating it must be for anyone who is contemplating murder.

PSYCHIATRIST:
A person who will listen to you as long as you don't make any sense.

My wife went shopping again. I can't believe some of the stuff that she would rather have than money.

She got a two-hundred-dollar coat. She said, "I can wear it with the collar turned up, or I can turn it down." I said, "Turn it down!"

An old Texas rancher dies and leaves the entire ranch to his only son. One day later the bank forecloses on the ranch.
The son says, "Well...Dad said that the ranch would be mine one day."

A Texan is in the Niagara Falls area. One of the locals points to the Falls and says, "I bet you haven't got anything like this in Texas."
The Texan says, "Nope. But we've got some plumbers who could fix it."

The plumber arrives to fix a leak and opens his large canvas tool bag. The bag is totally overflowing with money that pours all over the floor. There are twenty, fifty and hundred dollar bills everywhere

As he is stuffing all the money back into the big bag, the plumber says, "Can you believe this? I brought the wrong bag."

Just how important you are on the job depends on whether you're asking for a day off, or a raise.

Patrick Henry pointed out that taxation without representation is bad. Personally, I think it's become a real disaster even with representation.

What's new? There's a pharmaceutical company that has developed a pill that lowers your IQ for a couple hours. You take it before watching TV.

My neighbor's wife was complaining that he sits in front of their TV with nothing on. I asked her why he doesn't put something on.
She said, "He can't. The TV is broken."

My wife told me that the neighbors now allow their kids to play Jacks. Allow? I didn't know that kids even wanted to play Jacks anymore.
My wife said, "You're thinking of the wrong Jacks. The game they play involves their allowance, and requires jacks or better to open."

Toilet training a child has always been largely a matter of pot luck.

Personally, I like newspapers better than television. Try taking a nap with a television laying on your face.

There is something worse than a flooded basement. A flooded attic.

It's now to the point that, to be different, you've go to act normal.

MARRIAGE COUNSELOR TO COUPLE: "For starters, stop referring to each other as: 'Bozo' and 'Meathead.'"

I'm the first to admit that there are things I don't know about women. For example, I always thought that as women got older they turned blonde.

———————

They always say blondes are more desirable than brunettes and redheads. Well, my wife has been all three and I didn't notice any difference.

———————

When we were newlyweds she told me that I had this really great chin, so over the years I've grown another one, and she hates it.

———————

My wife felt compelled to tell me I've got the same stupid personality had when she married me. She said, "Only then I thought it was cute."

———————

She was an awful cook back then. One time the neighbor's dog got sick, and they called our house to see if maybe she had fed it something.

———————

I'm not kidding. She was a bad cook. She considered toast a hot meal.

———————

My neighbor took a fall. His foot got all tangled up on some great big cumbersome object that got in his way. Probably his other foot.

———————

Two cockroaches are eating lunch in the bottom of a filthy garbage can. One starts talking about the people that moved into the big house across the street. He says, "I hear they've cleaned out under the refrigerator. They cleaned under the sink. And you won't even recognize the basement. The place is absolutely spotless."
The other cockroach looks at him and says, "Could we please talk about something else while we're eating!"

———————

The doctor put me on this diet. He says I need to change my eating habits. For starters he thinks that I shouldn't eat so much bread with my meals. How does he expect me to sop up the gravy?

———————

He asked if I exercise. I said, "At my age all I exercise is caution."

TIP FOR THE HANDYMAN:
The best time to fix something is whenever your wife tells you to.

Our sewer was clogged and I couldn't get a plumber so I dug out all of the crud myself. Now I know why plumbers don't bite their nails.

Children brighten up a home...because they never turn off the lights.

It's no wonder parents often cry at weddings. They're very expensive.

A used car salesman tries to close a sale with: "We could let you have this beauty for eight thousand dollars. Buy it today for eight thousand, drive it for a bit, and I guarantee you won't sell it for ten thousand."
The guy buys it. He drives it and it's a lemon. He returns to the lot and reminds the salesman of the guarantee. He says, "You told me that if I drove this thing awhile I wouldn't sell it for ten thousand dollars."
The salesman says, "That's correct. You didn't, did you?"

Library studies reveal that most novels that aren't dirty are dusty.

Do you realize there are now more deductions on the average paycheck than there are in a Sherlock Holmes movie.

My wife and I read in moderation, but when it comes to the checkbook, neither one of us can put it down until it's finished.

We play cards with an unusual couple. He's crude and she's cross-eyed. Every time she gives him a dirty look she gets me.

They've now come out with an electric blanket that has three controls. It's for married couples who have a dog.

OVERHEARD AT THE BOWLING ALLEY:
"Somebody said that Fred was fired. What happened?"

"Let me put it this way. Do you know what foremen do all day?"

"Sure. They walk around and watch everyone work."

"That's right. Everyone thought Fred was a foreman."

At the high school prom a freshman boy asks a senior girl for a dance, but she shoots him down. She says, "No way. I never dance with a child."

So he shoots back, "Sorry. I didn't realize you're pregnant."

I read somewhere that robbers and muggers in Washington, D.C. now try to do most of the robbing and mugging during the day. They are afraid to be out on the D.C. streets at night, carrying that much money.

Two hunters drive to a farm. One stays in the car while the other goes up to the farm house. He asks the farmer, "Can we hunt on your land?"

The farmer says, "You can hunt here, but do me a favor. My horse is sick and must be put away. I can't shoot it. Would you shoot it for me?"

The hunter says, "I know how you feel. I'll shoot the horse for you." The hunter decides to pull a prank on his pal. He says, "The farmer was a real jerk. We can't hunt here. I'm so mad. I'm gonna shoot his horse." And he shoots it. Then he hears another shot from behind him. He turns and sees his friend with a smoking rifle saying, "I got his bull too."

At a party a physician is cornered by a boring man telling about every ache and pain he has, and has ever had. It goes on for a very long time. Eventually the physician notices someone across the room who is yawning. He says, "Look at that. I think that guy is eavesdropping on you."

At my house I say anything I please...because nobody listens anyway.

At an airport phone booth a guy waits for a friend who is on the phone for a very long time without saying a word. He finally asks, "Who the heck would keep you on hold this long?" His friend covers the mouthpiece with his hand and whispers, "I'm not on hold. I'm talking to my wife."

———

Talk about embarrassing. I fell asleep on a flight to Vegas recently. The woman next to me began poking me. I can't blame her because my head had slid over and it was resting on her shoulder. I think I was snoring. And I know I was drooling.

———

I sleep a lot. I gave up just about everything else. All I do is nap. And I still don't feel good.

———

One time I was really sick. I didn't sleep all night. It was that bad. My wife was up too. She was in the den reading my life insurance policy.

———

I know my wife is sadistic. She laughs when she peels onions.

———

OVERHEARD AT THE BEAUTY SALON:
"Lenny says he gave me the best years of his life. It's got me worried. What's coming up?"

———

We know that Newton discovered gravity when an apple fell on his head. But it is not well known that, after being hit on the head by the apple, Newton's first thoughts didn't involve gravity. They involved gratitude. He was thankful that he wasn't sitting under a coconut tree.

———

Much of the trouble in the country today is due to people who feel the need to let their conscience be your guide.

———

If there's anything to the theory of evolution, Americans will someday develop very powerful trigger fingers.

———

The latest conspiracy theory involves big corporations. Supposedly the nation's corporations banded together to control the content and quality of the programming on daytime TV. It's part of a plan to punish employees who stay home when they're not really sick.

———

OVERHEARD AT THE LAUNDROMAT:

"Marriage is a lot like getting a telephone call at two in the morning. First there's the ring. Then you wake up."

I can't win. When I'm away from home, I can't get my wife on the phone. When I'm home, I can't get her off the phone.

My neighbor says he can find numbers a lot faster now. He just noticed that the phone book lists them in alphabetical order.

This is the same guy who says he once missed getting a hole-in-one by only five strokes.

It seems whenever I go to a ball game, I get seated in the same place. Right between the vendors and their best customer.

A guy goes up to the desk at a hotel in a small southern town and asks the desk clerk, "If I take a room, what's there to do around here?"

The desk clerk says, "If you don't fancy watchin' the TV in your room, y'all can go downstairs. There's swimmin' in the basement."

So the guy checks in, but later on he is back at the desk complaining, "I've been down there four times. There ain't no women in the basement."

How embarrassing. The party invitation plainly said, "Black tie only." When I got there, everyone was wearing suits too.

My wife is upset again so I said, "I give up. What did I do wrong now?" She got laryngitis telling me.

The way she finds fault, you'd think there was a reward.

They say: "No man can serve two masters." This certainly isn't true if you've got a wife and a grown daughter.

I toss and turn at night, worrying about things I shouldn't worry about. What if "Stop & Shop" were to merge with "A & P." The possible number of acceptable new name combinations is limited. I think "Stop & A" is okay.

My neighbor's wife got him to take one of those speed reading courses. Now he rarely goes into the wrong restroom.

Is he a beauty or what? He's the kind of person who likes to eat and run. This doesn't surprise me. I've seen the way he tips.

What a guy! Once he was bragging about his seven-year football career. When I asked what college he went to, he said, "This was in high school."

I guess he could run and he could kick, but he couldn't pass.

OVERHEARD AT A BOWLING ALLEY:
"I heard that your fiancée dumped you."
"Yup. She found out about my rich uncle."
"So what if you have a rich uncle?"
"So now she's my aunt."

Exercise sensibly. Start slowly. You're probably not ready for jogging if you can't reach down and tie your own sneakers.

This flu season I've finally learned that Pepto Bismol actually works. Where I got confused in the past is...I was using it as a gargle.

Advice for couples planning a wedding: "Invite only people who are already married. That way the wedding gifts will be clear profit."

The other night I asked my neighbor what he did before he got married. He said, "Anything I wanted to."

He wrote to one of those advice-to-the-lovelorn type columnists asking, "Why do women close their eyes when they kiss."
She wrote back saying, "If you'll send me your picture, I may be better able to answer your question."

I'm a terrible speller. My wife said, "When you're in doubt, you should use a dictionary." It doesn't work. I'm never in doubt.

My wife and I work very hard to make our marriage last. We feel there are too many quitters. We've decided to make ours a fight to the finish.

SONG TITLE: She Tried To Kiss Me In The Fog And Mist.

COLLEGE FRESHMAN TO ROOMMATE:
"I have to do an essay on the importance of making your own decisions. What do you think I should write?"

Who would have thought the day would come when money saved in some old coffee can would earn about the same interest as the money in a bank CD?

Talk about losers. A guy in New York was worried he would get mugged if he walked home...so he ran. It didn't help. He caught up to a mugger.

There is one way even a big loser can wake up rich—if he is the loser in a world championship heavyweight boxing match.

Hard as he tries, a manager is not able to get any fifteen round boxing matches for his fighter. The manager is interviewed by reporters asking, "He's not even ranked, why do you insist on a fifteen round fight?"
The manager explains, "My guy ain't too good in short fights."
Unable to get any fifteen round matches, the manager eventually agrees to take a four round fight. But the fight doesn't even last the entire four rounds. His fighter is knocked out cold, early in the very first round.
After the fight the reporters ask the manager, "What went wrong?"
He says, "I told you. My guy ain't no good in short fights."

The guest on a TV talk show talked about studies that ranked the IQ of people in various parts of the U.S. I said, "How many super-smart

people do you think there are in this part of the country?"
My wife said, "One less than YOU think there are."

There are two ways to avoid divorce. Stay single, or stay married.

After years of always getting her own way, my daughter was eventually able to write her diary in advance.

FROM OUR MAIL BAG:
One reader writes to inform us that she found three spelling errors in last week's paper. She said, "You folks need a dictionary."
Well, Miss Smartypants, we may need a dictionary, but you need glasses. There were twenty-seven spelling errors in last week's paper.

OUR THOUGHT FOR THE DAY:
If you add just five new words a month to your vocabulary, before long your friends will start wondering who the heck you think you are.

The doctor says, "You seem to be a fairly healthy guy, but I think you should try to get a little sun."
The guy says, "I'll see what I can do. So far we've got all girls."

I know the honeymoon is over. My wife started sleeping with a stun-gun under her pillow.

Sometimes I think I'm funny and my wife doesn't. Like the time we went out on her birthday. As a joke I asked the guy at the piano bar to play "The Old Gray Mare She Ain't What She Used To Be."

My uncle is working on his second dynamite-powered dragster. The first one was fast, but he couldn't get all the parts to go in one direction.

I swear this one is true. One time I stopped at a roadside restaurant. A handwritten note on the menu recommended Cherry Crisps. Sounded good, so I ordered a cup of coffee, and a Cherry Crisp. Yuk! Now I know what they do with their stale Cherry Danish.

The teacher says, "This essay on 'Our Dog' is word for word the same as the one your brother handed in last year."

The kid shrugs and says, "It's the same dog."

The boss pulls an employee aside and says, "You were too sick to come to work yesterday, but you weren't too sick to go out and play golf."

The employee says, "I have no idea what makes you think that I was out playing golf. I didn't play golf. And I've got the fish to prove it."

The stress of modern life finally causes a guy to go off the deep end, and he begins to think that he's President Clinton. Daily he makes calls to various federal offices and to many heads of state around the world. His wife persuades him to see a psychiatrist. She says, "You need help."

After several months of hypnotherapy, the doctor says, "You are cured. Your delusions are over. You are no longer President Clinton."

The guy says, "Wow! What am I gonna tell Hillary?"

I have only got one wish for the new year. I wish this year's troubles last only as long as last year's resolutions lasted.

What do I do? On December 28th I got a great big box in the mail marked: "Do not open until Christmas."

I told my wife, "I talked to most of the neighbors and every one of them said that they got lots of stuff for Christmas this year."

She said, "Really? That's good. That means there will probably be some really great garage sales next summer."

The jury from a small town courthouse marches back into the courtroom. They've reached a decision. The foreman stands and says, "We don't think that the defendant did it because he wasn't even there when it happened, but we think that he would have done it if he had the chance."

Years ago my uncle claimed to know the town like the back of his hand. He used to brag that he could find his way anywhere in town blindfolded. This eventually led to his demise when a friend challenged him to travel across the town blindfolded. He made it almost all the way, but when he stopped to scratch his back on a post, a passing firing squad shot him.

My neighbor had a really bad break during deer hunting season this year. He was behind a big tree when an eight point buck ran into the clearing. He said he instinctively leaned against the tree to keep himself steady. Then he took three quick shots, but by the time he was able to put the cap back onto the bottle, the deer had run off.

They took a trip to the Grand Canyon last year and he was showing off.
He ran right up to the edge and hollered, "Hey, everybody! Look at me."
His wife looked. Then she hollered, "Either you get away from the edge or let someone else carry the sandwiches."

I never eat hash. I won't eat it in a restaurant because I don't know what all might be in it. And I won't eat it at home because I do know.

Regarding the article in last week's paper that suggested it's foolish to leave large sums of money around the house: One reader writes to say, "It's not foolish. It's impossible."

Some people do some pretty foolish things. There's a guy in New Jersey who went without food for eight days. Isn't that stupid? He should have given his order to another waiter.

Scientists say that the world is made of protons, neutrons and electrons. Apparently they don't read the paper, or the list would also include morons.

I read an interesting item in the paper and showed it to my wife. I pointed to the article and said, "It says here that they caught the biggest hotel thief in the city of New York."
She asked, "What hotel did he run?"

In one city the city council members have made a New Year's resolution to drive the criminals out of town. Personally, I think they're being way too soft on the criminals. I'd make them walk.

A guy walks up to the owner of a store and says, "You probably don't remember me, but about five years ago I was broke. I came in here and asked you for ten dollars, and you gave it to me."

The store owner smiles and says, "Yes. I remember."

The guy says, "Are you still game?"

The neighbor woman was making lunch when she heard a noise on their front porch. Thinking that it was her husband, she yelled, "I'm in here, honey. I've been waiting for you."

For a few seconds there was no reply. Then a voice said, "Sorry, lady, I'm not your regular mailman."

HUSBAND TO WIFE:

"I'm not trying to be unpleasant, dear. I simply want to know why we're the only people in town who still get their milk delivered."

A guy spots his doctor in the mall. He stops him and says, "Six weeks ago when I was in your office, you told me to go home, get into bed and stay there until you called. But you never called."

The doctor says, "I didn't? Then what are you doing out of bed?"

The new father stands silently looking at the crib where his firstborn lies sleeping. For a moment his wife stands in the doorway, watching the tender scene. Then she tiptoes into the room. She puts her hand in his and softly says, "A penny for your thoughts."

He says, "I was just wondering how the heck they can make a crib like this for only sixty-five bucks."

A flock of Canadian geese lands in a large field. The head goose calls the geese together. He says, "From now on if you're going to pass, pass. But I've had all I can take of this constant honking."

Leonard is at the bedside of his business partner who's extremely ill. Realizing he only has moments to live, the partner confesses to Leonard, "Over the years I've stolen about four million dollars from the company. And I've sold vital information to our competition for several thousand. Mostly I need to confess that I have also been seeing your wife."

Leonard says, "Yes. I know."

His partner says, "You know?"

Leonard says, "Yes. That's why I poisoned you."

Once while I was golfing, I lost my money clip with sixty dollars in it. If the caddy hadn't helped me look for it, I think I would have found it.

My neighbor told me that some old busybody accused him of spending the entire day in a local tavern. When he denied it, she said, "You were too. Your car was parked in front of the tavern all day."

He explained, "Just because my car was parked in front of the tavern, does not mean I was in the tavern." She wouldn't listen, so that night he parked his car in front of her house.

The people who are most likely to be unfaithful in marriage are those who think they're too good to be true.

A group of church women hold their annual spring Flower Banquet at the same hotel where some boisterous heavy equipment salesmen hold their annual Victory Banquet. Through an error in the kitchen, the church women are served the heavily vodka-spiked watermelon that was special ordered for the salesmen's rowdy Victory Banquet.

The hotel manager panics. He says, "Somebody get that watermelon back before those ladies eat any of it."

The waiter says, "It's too late. They're already eating it."

The hotel manager says, "Did any of them say anything about it?"

The waiter says, "None of them has said anything, but most of them are putting the seeds in their purses."

A guy arrives at the Pearly Gates. St. Peter asks him, "Did you lead a good life while you were on earth?"

The guy says, "I was very good while I was on earth. I had my chances, but I always resisted temptation. I didn't drink. I didn't gamble. And I didn't chase with wild women or cheat on my wife. Check your records."

St. Peter says, "We'll take your word for it. We don't keep records."

As the guy enters, he sees that most of the men are playing this rather strange soccer type game, but he notices that they are not using a ball. They just take turns kicking each other. They kick themselves a lot too. There doesn't seem to be a point to the game, so the guy asks St. Peter, "What are they doing?"

Saint Peter says, "I don't know, but they've been doing it ever since they found out we don't keep records."

The plumber knocks on the front door of a house. When a woman answers, he says, "Did you call for a plumber?"

The woman says, "Yes, I did, but that was last December."

The plumber says, "Sorry for the mistake. I must have the wrong house. The people I'm looking for called last August."

My neighbor applied for a civil service job. One of the questions during the interview was: "Were you ever a part of any organization that planned to overthrow the government in Washington?"

My neighbor said, "Yes."

They were surprised. They said, "You were? What was the organization?"

My neighbor said, "The Republican Party."

GOLF TIP: Never play golf with anybody who writes down their score and then wipes their finger prints off the pencil.

A guy goes into a bar. The bartender says, "What's your pleasure?"

The guy says, "I guess I will have a scotch and a package of gum, please." He drinks the scotch and puts thirty-five cents on the counter.

The bartender says, "What's the thirty-five cents for?"

The guy says, "That's for the gum. I didn't come in here for a drink, but you asked me what my pleasure was, so I told you."

The bartender says, "That's just an expression." But the guy refuses to pay, and he's told to get out and never to come into the bar again.

A week later the guy returns. The bartender says, "Get out! I told you last week that you can't come in here anymore."

The guy says, "Last week? You must have me mixed up with someone else. I've just come back from several months out west."

The bartender looks him over and says, "Then you must have a double."

The guy says, "Well, thank you, I will. And a pack of gum, too, please."

OVERHEARD IN A MARRIAGE COUNSELOR'S OFFICE:
Before we were married, I talked and she listened. After we got married, she talked and I listened. Lately we both talk and the neighbors listen.

My neighbor took his wife out to a fancy restaurant. They each had lobster, two bottles of wine and a large dessert. As they sipped Brandy Alexanders afterwards, my neighbor said, "If my doctor saw me, he'd be rather upset."
His wife said, "Does he have you on some kind of diet?"
He said, "No. I still owe him a whole bunch of money."

She thinks he's an animal lover 'cause she heard that he put his shirt on a horse that was scratched.

A painter advertises in the paper that his paint jobs last ten years. A potential client says, "Are you sure your paint jobs last ten years?"
He says, "Yes, I am. I've been in the painting business for ten years and nobody has ever asked for a second job."

Last week we reported that archaeologists unearthed an old coin on the site of what was once a settler's home south of town. Turns out the coin is smooth on both sides, and they can't make heads or tails out of it.

They also unearthed an ancient sink...under a pile of ancient dishes.

A Hollywood producer is making a movie on the life of Abraham Lincoln. The film is historically accurate, but the story drags a little when it comes to its box office appeal. He calls the writers together and says, "We have got to punch-up the story line. I've got some ideas, but first you guys need to research everything you can find on Abraham Lincoln and see if he ever knew any woman who even remotely resembled Sharon Stone."

For a while it was a common practice for the various media to refer to the U.S. President by his initials. [FDR, JFK, LBJ] Political analysts now speculate that this is probably why Steven O. Bradford never ran.

Sometimes you just can't win! I was watching TV and my wife was doing a crossword puzzle. She asked, "What is a female sheep...three letters?"

I said, "Ewe." She gave me a dirty look and left the room.

I stayed at a five star hotel, and tried to get change for a dollar at the front desk. I learned that, at a five star hotel, a dollar is change.

My neighbor said he went into business. I asked what kind of business he went into. He said, "It's a partnership."

I said, "Did you have to put in much money?"

He said, "No. My partner put in the money. I put in the experience."

There is a good chance that, in time, my neighbor will have the money, and his partner will have the experience.

CLIMBING THE CORPORATE LADDER. RULE #247:

When climbing the corporate ladder, kiss the feet of the person above you, while stepping on the fingers of the person below you.

Grandma is babysitting Junior for a couple days. The first morning she makes oatmeal for him. Grandma sets it down and asks if he likes butter. Junior says, "Yes." She asks if he likes sugar. Junior says, "Yes."

Grandma says, "Of course, you like milk too." Junior says that he does. Grandma puts some sugar, a little butter and some milk on the oatmeal and gives it to Junior, but he won't eat it. She says, "When I asked you if you like sugar, butter and milk, you said you did. Why don't you eat?"

Junior says, "You didn't ask if I like oatmeal."

Some census takers stop at the home of Emma Brown. She answers all the questions, but when they ask her how old she is, Emma is rather reluctant. She says, "You already talked with Mr. and Mrs. Hill who live next door. I'm as old as they are."

That night, after thinking about her reply, Emma lies awake worrying that they may have put down: "Emma Brown is as old as the Hills."

A little old woman on a bus tour of Washington, D.C. gets separated from the rest of her group while they're inside the Pentagon. In a claustrophobic panic she wanders the maze of hallways for nearly an hour. Then she sees a house phone sitting on the counter in one of the offices. She picks it up and gets the switchboard operator. She says, "How do I get outside?"

The operator says, "Dial nine."

If the world is getting smaller, why do the postal rates keep going up?

A newly hired bank teller complains to his wife: "They are very strict. When you add up the deposits, if the total is wrong, it's all wrong."

A wife explains to her husband, "Just as many people drown in bathtubs as drown in swimming pools." She adds, "And that's the only reason there was a lifeguard in the bathtub."

A borrower, approved for a five-thousand-dollar loan, asks the banker, "Could you add an extra five hundred dollars to the loan?"

The banker asks, "What for?"

The guy says, "I bet a friend five hundred bucks you'd turn me down."

A New York couple visits Vienna and goes to the museum which has Beethoven's piano on display. The guy reaches over and plays a few notes, approvingly nods to his wife, then looks at the guide and says, "I suppose you get a lot of famous musicians who come to see this thing."

The guide says, "Yes, sir. In fact just before the great Paderewski died, he traveled all the way to Vienna just to see this piano."

The New Yorker jokes, "I bet Paderewski played it better than I did."

The attendant says, "No. He didn't feel worthy to touch it."

As they march off on their twenty-mile hike, an army recruit asks a friend, "Why are those guys cheering us?"

The friend explains, "They're not cheering us. Those are the guys who don't have to go."

The doctor gave me a physical. He says I'm definitely not anorexic.

In his own way my neighbor, the outdoorsman, is doing his part to save the forests. He shot a woodpecker.

A Chicago man about to retire, decides to build a house in the country. He finds a very quaint little town that is many miles away from Chicago. He shows the plans to the local carpenter asking, "Can you build this?"

The carpenter studies the blueprint and says, "Oh-oh! Someone's really got these plans messed up. But I can draw up some new plans for you."

The guy says, "I hired one of the best architectural firms in Chicago to draw these plans. If you want the job...you will use these plans."

The carpenter says, "Well, okay. But I warn you. If you use these plans, you're gonna end up with two bathrooms."

Every morning the guy who blows the noon siren calls the radio station to get the correct time, yet the noon siren is usually off by as much as fifteen minutes each day. Sometimes it's fast. Sometimes it's slow.

People start to complain so the guy decides to contact the radio station. They say, "No wonder. We've been setting our clock by the noon siren."

Spring break can't come soon enough. School kids need time to rearm.

CLEVER LINES TO SAY TO A STATE TROOPER:
If you should ever get pulled over by the state patrol and the trooper says, "Do you know why I stopped you?"

Pretend to think about it. Then say, "I'm the only one you can catch?"

Ladies, you can profit from your husbands' mistakes. Have a yard sale.

Last night someone broke into my neighbor's home and took his glasses. He gave a description to the police. Police are now looking for a large, fuzzy, grayish blob.

Anyone who watches the news on television can see that our streets are not safe. Our neighborhoods are not safe. Even our schools are not

180

safe. Then they see the television commercials and realize that the only place they can expect to have complete protection is under their arms.

I envy those people who lived during the 1930's. All they had to fear was fear itself.

My neighbor says he never gets mad when he plays golf. He says that he has learned to laugh when he makes a lousy shot. The last time he played he laughed 37 times.

On my birthday my wife said, "I have a little surprise."
I said, "Where is it?"
She said, "Just a minute, I'll go put it on."

A farmer goes into an implement dealer's showroom with a shoe box full of hundred dollar bills. He says, "I'd like to buy a tractor. How much?"
The salesman says, "I know what the monthly payment is, but I'm afraid that I don't know what the actual selling price is."
The bookkeeper says, "I don't know how to record a cash transaction."
And the sales manager says, "I am kind of leery about the entire thing. We don't even have a credit report."

OVERHEARD IN A BARBERSHOP:
My wife really does love me. I stayed home from work one day last week because I was sick. Whenever a mailman or delivery man came, she shouted, "My husband's home. My husband's home."

A boxing manager attempts to boost his fighter's confidence by saying: "Don't worry...if this guy was any good, he wouldn't be fighting you.

Question: What is the favorite hobby of most apartment managers?
Answer: Collecting security deposits.

The neighbors were having an argument. She said, "Do you realize that everything you do annoys me. You annoy me all day long. Wait. I take that back. It's worse than that. You annoy me all day long, and at night you snore."

———

Next week we'll answer the letter received from a reader who wondered: "Am I legally married if the shotgun wasn't loaded?"

———

The father says, "You ask so many questions. Do you know what would've happened if I would have asked so many questions when I was a kid?"
The son says, "You'd be able to answer some of mine now?"

———

AT THE SCENE OF A SHOOT-OUT IN THE OLD WEST
Bad-guy, "All right you scum-ball. Pick a number between one and ten."
Good-guy, "I pick three."
Bad-guy, "Okay, I'll count to three, and on three, turn and fire."
Good-guy, "That sounds fair enough to me."
Bad-guy, "Here goes. One!...Two!...[BANG!]"
Good-guy, "Ouch! Hey...you said to turn and fire on *three*."
Bad-guy, "Right. *Your number* was three. I picked two."

———

CADDY: The kid behind a golfer who didn't see the ball either.

MORE LAUGHS PER DOLLAR THAN YOU THOUGHT POSSIBLE! WELL WITHIN NEARLY ANY BUDGET BECAUSE...

Ron speaks from twelve to twenty times per month, to groups as small as several dozen, or as large as several thousand.

If you are interested in booking a speaking engagement, contact:

Ron Dentinger
P.O. Box 115
Dodgeville, WI 53533
(608) 935-2417

To order a copy of this book call Kendall/Hunt Publishing Company at 1-800-228-0810, or send $15.95 plus $3.00 for shipping and handling to:

Kendall/Hunt Publishing Company
P. O. Box 1840
4050 Westmark Drive
Dubuque, IA 52004-1840